Happy belated birthday
Patience,

Frank

T4-AJY-924

A THEORY ON THE
NATURE OF HUMANITY

A THEORY ON THE NATURE OF HUMANITY

By
James Blake Thomas

Published by
James Blake Thomas and
ACADEMY OF HUMAN STUDIES
through

REDACTIONS
UNLIMITED

1986

Library of Congress Catalogue Card Number: 86-90039
International Standard Book Number: 0-9616285-0-2

Additional copies available from
  James Blake Thomas and
  Academy of Human Studies
  2946 Mt. Hope
  Okemos, Michigan 48864

CONTENTS

III: COMMENTARY, *continued*

PREFACE

I have always understood that the publication of someone's life work is a reporting of things done—things done with purpose, effort, plan, direction, and demonstrable results. My writings in these pages, these musings of mine, most certainly do not represent a life work. Rather, what I have written here reflects my life experiences—experiences of being and exploring without conscious purpose; without effort, plan, or direction; and certainly without demonstrable results in their scientific sense.

In reflecting on my own life experiences I understand that, collectively and individually, they are quite ordinary, but it is precisely in their commonness that I have discovered what is to me the very truth of being human. My understanding of this truth emerged in October 1984 following a time spent in solitude and intimacy on the coast of Maine. While the understanding became evident to me at a specific time, I can see in retrospect that what is now understood was there all the while. This understanding, this truth, might well have come to me much earlier if my experiences of being and of exploring in being had not been so obscured by my doing. I had been given to doing "important" things as a student, teacher, researcher, physician, psychiatrist, landowner, parent, and spouse.

And in my efforts to be successful, to be good enough at these life works, I had all too often ignored my very being. Many of the views and ideas presented in this book emerged from my experience in *doing* psychotherapy with patients as a psychiatrist. As you may come to see, the *doing* more often than not clouded the experience.

The substance of the book itself, *A Theory on the Nature of Humanity,* was arrived at through a process of exploration and discovery. This process occurred primarily in my consulting room and it occurred over a period of time, the exact parameters of which are not precisely known. There was no a priori plan or design for the exploration, and there was no written record of the journey. What follows is my recollection of that process of exploration and discovery, and a formal statement of the theory.

James Blake Thomas
February 1986

ACKNOWLEDGMENTS

The ideas and views put forth in this book are wholly mine, and I take full responsibility for them. At the same moment I wish to express my heartfelt appreciation to those persons whom I met along the way in my journey of discovery—persons who, each in their own unique way, contributed to my experiences beyond measure.

To my patients for allowing, encouraging, and at times demanding me to listen.

To those many whom I have never met face to face but who have enriched my life through their writings. To name all of them would be an impossible task, but here I would name: Dietrich Bonhoeffer, Martin Buber, Thomas Hardy, Kai Munk, John A. T. Robinson, Adlai Stevenson, and Alfred North Whitehead.

To Kathleen M. Schoonmaker of Redactions Unlimited for her editorial skills, for being gentle with my fractured prose, and for tolerating my idiosyncratic ways.

To Father John Mitman and Drs. Arnold Berkman, Jacque Miller, and Margaret A. Thomas for their patience, perseverance, and encouragement in listening to me and in questioning me as these ideas emerged in spoken and written form.

Finally, to all those dear souls who encouraged or at least allowed me to be and to explore freely. To Amy, Anne, Blake, Blanche, Brandt, Brevard, Christopher, David, Edith, Herbert, John, John, Margaret, and Paul.

Dedicatio

DEVS · ES · SVM

I

EXPLORATION

HE UNIVERSE EXISTS. IT IS. The solar system, with the sun and the moon and the planet earth, exists. It is. Upon the face of the earth oceans and continents exist. They are. And within the oceans and upon the land plants exist that grow and bear fruit and die. They are. Animals grow and bear fruit and die. They exist. They are. Of the animals, many have the capacity to learn and to remember and to respond conditionally to the world around them.

Human beings exist. We are. We grow and bear fruit and die. We have the capacity to learn, to remember, and to respond conditionally to the world around us. But being human goes beyond this. We are set apart from the other creatures of the earth. We, as human beings, have the capacity for reason and logic and directed thought. These capacities lead us to being curious, lead us to an unending quest for an understanding of the world around us and of ourselves. We seek to understand the universe and ourselves not merely to know that the universe exists and that we exist. Human beings transcend mere existence; we experience an essence of life, an essence that emerges from our unique perceptions of the world around us, from our values and tastes, from our emotions and desires, and from our fantasies and impulses. As human beings we not only experience an essence that exceeds mere existence; we may also convey the nature of that experience to others through language. I can see that you exist as a human being, just as I can see that a rock or a bird or a tree exists. And you can see that I exist. But it is only through language that I can convey to you my own human nature, my essence of life, just as it is only through language that I may understand your experience of life. "Language...is the instrument of all our distinctly human development, of everything in which we go beyond the other animals."[1]

In the course of Western civilization, at least since the time of Plato and perhaps before, three questions have constantly assailed our human curiosity, our desire to understand. These three questions are: What is the nature of the universe? What is the nature of Man? What is Man's role in the universe? Exploration for an understanding of the universe has led to the development of the natural sciences. Exploration for an understanding of the nature of Man—the nature of ourselves—has led to the development of the

1. I. A. Richards, *The Philosophy of Rhetoric* (1936), cited in Robert Burchfield, *The English Language* (Oxford: Oxford University Press, 1985), p. xiii.

humanities. Exploration for an understanding of Man's role in the universe has led to the development of the social sciences. The liberal arts tradition addresses these three questions as the focus of its scholarly inquiries and accepts these three questions as having equal merit.

The theory on the nature of humanity presented herein is an attempt to bring further clarity to understanding the question of the nature of Man. It is worthy of note that the theory derives from a liberal arts tradition rather than from a circumscribed discipline; equally worthy of note is that the theory was arrived at by exploration and discovery rather than by scientific experimentation based on formulated hypotheses. To understand this process of exploration and discovery it is necessary to understand the background for exploration, as I will now describe.

SCIENCE VERSUS THE HUMANITIES

Despite civility and charity, the sciences and the humanities have long faced each other from opposite sides of a seemingly unfathomable chasm, a chasm first evident to me during my undergraduate days at Wabash College in the early 1950s. There, the science majors, myself included, when taking the obligatory humanities courses for the liberal arts curriculum, persistently appraised the humanities with interrogations such as: Philosophy, religion, languages, literature, art, music, and drama are duly fascinating, but of what use are they? They are not scientific. They are not measurable. What are their laws and theories and formulae? What do they have that is comparable with the laws of thermodynamics or the theory of relativity or the theory of numbers or the principles of genetics?

There also the humanities majors, when taking the obligatory science courses, persistently assessed the sciences with questions such as: Biology, mathematics, chemistry, and physics are, beyond much doubt, measuring and scientific, but of what use is a godless science without values or morals or ethics? What have the marvels of science given us other than air pollution (humanities majors always found our laboratories odious), water pollution, and the threat of nuclear extinction?

These two views seem, without contention, valid; no readily available way appears to reconcile them. The natural sciences, in the quest to understand the question regarding the nature of the universe, have observed, measured, learned—and led to a body of knowledge and facts. The humanities, in the quest to understand the question of the nature of Man, have depended on experience and language. A chasm yawns between the disciplines. There is no common ground.

PSYCHIATRY VERSUS THE SCIENCES AND THE HUMANITIES

For some time following my obligatory liberal arts experience, I remained on the scientific side of the chasm, first as a medical student, then as a doctoral candidate in human anatomy, and later as a faculty member teaching and conducting research in human embryology. Eventually I came to the discipline of psychiatry, whereupon I found myself no longer on the scientific edge but rather in the abyss itself. My medical colleagues, many of whom wrongly accuse themselves of being "scientific," state that psychiatry lacks a scientific basis and cannot provide predictable and reproducible results—an observation essentially the same as that which the science majors at Wabash made of the humanities and, in my view, equally valid. Those of my colleagues who are therapists but who do not come from a medical tradition—psychologists, some psychoanalysts, some priests and rabbis and social workers, some of whom wrongly accuse themselves of being "humanists"—state that medicine and science have no place in psychotherapy. They use as justification the same criticisms that the humanities majors at Wabash made of the sciences: that values, morals, or ethics must be involved. Again, in my view, this observation is valid.

From these purviews, psychiatrists are "neither fish nor flesh nor good red-herring."[2] They do not look across the chasm, but are rather *in* it and looked down upon by both "scientists" and "humanists." But what a marvelous place to explore.

---

2. John Dryden, Epilogue to *The Duke of Guise*.

THE MEDICAL MODEL

In the simplest, and thus most revealing, model of medicine the patient first presents to a physician a symptom or group of symptoms. At this point, the patient is primarily, and in some cases exclusively, desirous of finding a path to the earliest possible moment in the future when the symptoms will no longer exist. The physician's first responsibility is to *understand* the problem, which is done by noting clinical signs, taking a history, doing a physical examination, and ordering laboratory studies—all forms of scientific measurement. Once the problem is understood, usually in the form of a diagnosis, the physician's second responsibility is to formulate a treatment plan and offer it to the patient. It is then the responsibility of the patient to accept or reject the plan. If the treatment plan is accepted, it becomes the door to the desired point in the future when the patient will be free of symptoms. Thus, the process progresses from symptoms to understanding to treatment to "cure."

In this model it is not necessary for the patient to understand the problem or the specifics of the treatment; it is only necessary for the patient to accept or decline the offered treatment. That is not to say that it is necessary for the patient *not* to understand, only that it is not necessary for the patient to understand.

EXAMPLE: A patient reports a cough of five days' duration. The cough produces copious amounts of thick, yellow mucous, is intermittent, is worse on retiring, has interfered with sleep, and has led to generalized fatigue and malaise. The physician must now make sense out of the problem, must now *understand* it. Is the cough secondary to bronchitis or pneumonia? Is it caused by *Streptococcus pneumoniae, Hemophilus influenzae, Pseudomonas aerogenosa, Mycobacterium tuberculosis,* adenovirus, *Mycoplasm pneumoniae,* or some other offending organism or perhaps some other noninfectious condition? Clinical exploration should lead to the answer. Let it be given that the infecting organism is *Mycoplasm pneumoniae;* then the treatment plan might be for the patient to take 500 mgm of tetracycline three times daily for a total of ten days. The patient now has a door to that specific time in the future when he or she will be free of symptoms. The patient does not have to know anything about the *Mycoplasm* organism or about the pharmacology of tetracycline.

A corollary to this model is that it is generally considered dangerous, and in many cases unethical, for a physician to treat symptoms without *first* understanding the problem.

EXAMPLE: A patient presents a symptom of excruciating abdominal pain with an acute onset. It would be quite simple to offer relief from the pain by administration of a narcotic analgesic such as morphine. But to do so without first exploring the nature of the underlying problem, e.g., appendicitis, kidney stones, perforated duodenal ulcer, pancreatitis, ruptured ectopic pregnancy, or gastroenteritis, may result in tragedy.

THE PSYCHOTHERAPY MODEL

The psychotherapy model is essentially the same as the medical model. The patient brings symptoms in the form of anxiety, depression, agitation, or generalized human despair, and, as in the medical model, wants a pathway to some future point when he or she will be free of distressing symptoms. It is now the therapist's responsibility to *understand* the problem, with such understanding being based, in the main, on existing psychodynamic and psychoanalytic theories. Understanding the problem is not by scientific measurement, as in the medical model, but rather by the process of psychotherapy in which the therapist and the patient explore the symptoms in an effort to uncover their genesis. Thus, the treatment plan is also the process of psychotherapy which, again unlike the medical model, requires the patient to understand the problem and to be part of the treatment. If the patient can actively participate in the process of psychotherapy and, through exploration, come to understand the problem, then the symptoms should abate or disappear. If the symptoms are secondary to dementia, delerium, or psychosis, including schizophrenia, then the patient will not be able to participate in the psychotherapeutic process.

A corollary to this model is that it would be equally as dangerous as it was in the previously described medical model to treat symptoms without first understanding the problem. Yet psychiatry currently comes very close to doing just that. The fields of pharmacotherapy and behavior therapy offer treatments aimed at symptom reduction, but without a scientific basis comparable to that demanded of medicine in general, and without heed to psychodynamic theories. Paul Willner, in his scholarly paper on a theory of psychopharmacology, sums this up succinctly: "There is no doubt that research into the effects of antidepressant drugs on noradrenergic systems has led to fundamental advances in our understanding of neuronal functioning. Whether it has told as much about depression, however, is a question that still remains to be answered."[3]

PSYCHOTHERAPY IN
QUEST OF THE ANSWER

Psychoanalytic and psychodynamic theories are nothing more or less than attempts to answer the age-old question, What is the nature of Man? Although psychotherapists are properly seen as clinicians offering treatment for human suffering, they are in fact struggling daily with the lack of any clear and

3. Paul Willner, "Drugs, Biochemistry and Conscious Experience: Toward a Theory of Psychopharmacology," *Perspectives in Biology and Medicine,* 28:1, 49–64.

satisfactory answer to the question. Psychotherapy can, therefore, never truly work until such time as the nature of Man is fully understood. If, as therapists, we do not in fact understand the nature of Man, then surely we cannot possibly understand the individual patient. It is my view that psychotherapy offers both solace and an opportunity for personal growth for a significant number of people. Although it begs the certainty of either *Mycoplasm pneumoniae* or tetracycline, psychotherapy can be clinically beneficial, but currently psychotherapies based on psychodynamic and psychoanalytic theories are on ground as uncertain as that on which psychopharmacological and behavioral therapies are based.

What, to me, is more important is to recognize that the process of psychotherapy offers a dynamic human arena in which the nature of Man can be fully explored by patient and therapist in unadorned privacy in the chasm twixt the sciences and the humanities. Sadly, that exploration is often impeded when therapists, myself included, categorically accept their own knowledge and guesses as the truth.

KNOWLEDGE VERSUS TRUTH

Our human capacity for reason, logic, and directed thought leads to an unending quest for an understanding of the world around us and of ourselves. And, as noted earlier, this intrinsic human curiosity leads to the seminal questions regarding the nature of the universe, the nature of Man, and Man's role in the universe.

The closest we can get to understanding, to the truth, is to make sense of things, which, as I will note later, can only be achieved through exploration. When something makes sense to us individually it becomes a personal truth; when something makes sense to us collectively it becomes a collective truth. It follows that not to be able to make sense of the world around us or ourselves is intolerable. Furthermore, when understanding is not immediately available to us, we tend to make guesses. These guesses, which are frequently automatic and necessary in the absence of understanding, take three basic forms: hypotheses, assumptions, and beliefs.

The first form of a guess is the hypothesis, most commonly associated with scientific inquiry. The hypothesis is a guess usually made in the midst of exploration that gives direction to further exploration. Here is a simple example: If one is lost in the forest and guesses that a town is to the north (hypothesis), then that is the direction chosen for further exploration.

The second form of the guess is the assumption, which offers (a) a time out from exploration until such time as exploration can be resumed, or (b) a permanent discontinuation of exploration of events deemed to be of little importance.

EXAMPLE A: A person makes arrangements to meet a friend for dinner at a specific restaurant at 8:00 p.m. The person arrives at 7:50 p.m. and waits. At 8:15 p.m. the friend has not yet arrived. There is no possibility of an exploration for understanding because the truth has not yet arrived, so the person will probably make an assumption until further exploration is possible—namely, when the friend finally arrives. The menu of possible assumptions is very long indeed. The assumptions may range from "maybe they've been in an accident" (with attendant anxiety), to "maybe they're insensitive and don't really care that I have to wait" (with attendant resentment and anger), to "maybe they really don't want to spend time with me and are avoiding me" (with attendant uncertainty and discomfort), to "maybe this isn't the right restaurant" (with attendant anticipation of embarrassment).

Such assumptions are always guesses; they are never the same as understanding. Only when truth arrives in the form of the friend can exploration for understanding the truth begin. Tragically, many people live in a world of assumptions that they accept as the truth. As already noted, psychotherapists have not been immune to treating assumptions as truth, thus impeding exploration in search of an understanding of the nature of Man.

EXAMPLE B: If one is sitting in a public room, say a waiting room at an airport, and notices a person across the room who is tearful, then the assumption (guess) might be that the person feels sad. The only way to understand what the person is feeling (the truth) is through exploration (people cannot be understood by observation no matter how precise and scientific the observations are). But since the person observed is a stranger encountered in a public place, one can accept the assumption as close enough to the truth, which allows discontinuation of exploration of something deemed unimportant.

The third form of guess is a belief, or myth, which satisfies our need for understanding when further exploration seems impossible. Examples that require no further clarification are the belief that God created the universe, the belief that there is (or is not) a life after death, or the belief that there are other life forms in the universe.

That guesses—hypotheses, assumptions, and beliefs—derive from reasoned, logical exploration for the truth means that the guesses are, in and of themselves, reasonable and logical. But they are never the truth. Again, to accept guesses as the truth impedes or stops exploration.

Exploration and awareness lead to understanding, whereas learning leads to knowledge. Learning is an intellectual process involving reason, logic, and memory. I can learn "that is an apple" without exploring an apple, without touching or smelling or tasting an apple, and even without seeing an apple. I can learn "that is an apple" from a picture. Once I learn this, I have knowledge of the apple. Conversely, I can be aware of and explore an apple, thereby understanding the apple through my experience, and this may be done without learning "that is an apple." We can learn from others on the basis of their understanding, or even on the basis of their guesses, but this leads only to knowledge. Knowledge, like guesses, when accepted as understanding—as the truth—interferes with exploration.

> EXAMPLE: When I was taking a senior philosophy course in college (one of those obligatory humanities courses), I learned about Taoism, I achieved some level of knowledge, I was able to come up with a sufficient number of correct answers for the examinations. I knew about "the way of nothingness," and I learned that "the learned are not wise and the wise are not learned." But to me this all seemed to belong to a distant, mystical, Oriental world beyond my comprehension. I did not understand it; I simply *knew* about it. The way to understanding, or truth or wisdom or maturity, is to explore in the absence of knowledge and guesses, to explore from nothingness. The wisdom of our judicial system is based on (but not always practiced on the basis of) the same understanding: to determine the truth of the matter in court proceedings, the judge and jury must explore the facts and circumstances of the case "without prejudice,"

that is, without prior knowledge or guesses
(hypotheses, assumptions, or beliefs).

EXAMPLE: For many years, my teaching and
research interests were in the field of human embryology. I learned about human prenatal development and pregnancy and, eventually, wrote
a textbook on human embryology. To state that
I have more knowledge about pregnancy than
many or most women would be reasonable and
accurate, but I can never understand pregnancy
since I cannot explore or experience pregnancy.
I am learned about pregnancy, but I shall never
be wise about pregnancy.

Children, who have natural curiosity about themselves and the world around them and are unfettered
by knowledge or guesses, are pure explorers. They
pick up and examine things that adults would not
touch, and they smell and taste things that adults
choose to avoid. Given enough time, children,
through exploration, could eventually make as much
sense, or more, of the world and of the self as adults
have at their command. But life is finite, and learning
on the basis of *someone else's* understanding, is efficient.
While children are busy exploring, adults in the persons of parents, teachers, Uncle Joe, or grandmother
intervene, quite properly, to say "now it is time to
learn."

When learning begins, exploration has to be inter-
rupted. When a teacher says, "Today we are going

to learn that $2 + 2 = 4$," then it is time to learn, not
to explore. The explorers want to keep exploring and
ask, "How do you know $2 + 2 = 4$?" or "If $2 + 2
= 4$ then what does $4 + 4$ equal?" or "What does $2
+ 2 + 2$ equal?" or, simply, "Why?" For the teacher
to allow continued exploration would lead to chaos
and would interfere with learning; a time out from
exploration is necessary. That, in our society, time
out from exploration far too often becomes permanent
is a matter of casual observation. We are a society of
learned experts. Understanding and widsom are in
short supply.

At this point I will make explicit my wish that those
who might choose to read this monograph would
explore it and reach whatever understanding, whatever truth, might be available here. To learn about
or to have knowledge of this theory and its applications would, in my view, make mockery of my inten-
tions. This will, of course, require the reader to read
from nothingness. To quote from Lao-tze's *Tao Te
Ching,* "Along the way to knowledge, many things
are accumulated. Along the way to wisdom, many
things are discarded."[4]

LANGUAGE, WORDS, AND DEFINITIONS

Our ever-increasing understanding of the universe
comes from scientific observations, but understanding

4. In Benjamin Hoff, *The Way to Life* (New York: John Weatherhill,
Inc., 1981), p. 43.

human nature cannot be based on observation alone. While the natural sciences rely on observation for understanding the universe, the humanities must rely on language to understand the nature of humanity.

Language is defined as "the expression and communication of emotions and ideas between human beings by means of speech and hearing, the sounds spoken or heard being systematized and confirmed by usage among a given people over a period of time."[5] For human nature to be understandable, it must be expressed in language with words that are confirmed by common usage.

A word is defined as "a linguistic form that can meaningfully be spoken in isolation."[6] Therefore, to express ourselves so that our human nature may be understood we must use words that have meaning in isolation, words that have precise meaning. Any lack of clarity and definition in our expression of ourselves will, perforce, bring a lack of clarity and definition to the understanding of human nature. The exploration for understanding human nature is, in fact, an exploration of words. Since each of us experiences and is aware of our own human nature, then we should be capable of making that nature understandable to others with language.

Previous psychoanalytic and psychodynamic theo-

---

5. Funk & Wagnalls *Standard College Dictionary* (New York: Harcourt, Brace & World, Inc., 1963), p. 760.

6. Ibid., p. 1547.

ries have generated their own languages to *explain* human nature, but they have not generally offered any systematized, confirmed usage of the common, often imprecise, words that people use in expressing themselves. Further, much of the language of psychoanalytic and psychodynamic theories is based on therapists' observations and on their intellectual and logical evaluation of patients. One can explore the universe with observations and can make logical deductions about the nature of the universe on the basis of such observations, but these techniques do not serve the exploration for understanding human nature.

In my own exploration for understanding, I have focused on requesting clarity of definition of words used. This has provided my patients, friends, family, and myself with moments of consternation mitigated by amusement. On more than one occasion I have been reproached with statements such as "oh, that's just semantics." Semantics or no, it was in the pressing for exact meanings of words that exploration occurred.

EXAMPLE: It is quite common for people to express an experience of "feeling hurt." The following offers an example of the process of pursuing such an expression for clarity:
Statement: "I was really hurt by that."
Response: "What do you mean 'hurt'?"
Statement: "You know. I felt hurt."
Response: "I don't know. As a physician, when
    I hear the word *hurt* I associate that with cuts

and bruises and fractures. Is that what you
mean?"

Statement: "You know what I mean. Haven't
your feelings ever been hurt?"

Response: "I experience my feelings, but I can't
see them or touch them, so they can't be hurt
in the sense that I use the word *hurt*. However,
what I need to understand is how you use the
word, what it means to you. What does it
mean to you when you say you're 'hurt'?"

Statement: "Well, I'm not sure. I thought
everyone knew what that meant."

And so the process goes until the person is clearly
understandable.

Any understanding of human nature available in
this monograph has come from exploring the words
that people use in expressing themselves, in expressing
their human nature. As further background to the
theory on the nature of humanity, two words will
now be examined.

THE GOOD-EVIL DICHOTOMY

One belief about the nature of Man permeates the
thought and literature of Western civilization: namely,
that Man is constantly struggling with an intrinsic
dichotomy between good and evil. Specifically, this
derives from the Old Testament myth of Man's fall
from grace in the Garden of Eden and from the teachings of St. Paul in the New Testament. I also recall
reading and learning in a senior philosophy class that

"no part of human nature escaped the consequences of the Fall of Man, and his reason did not remain unimpaired...."[7]   Every   discipline   within   the humanities generally accepts this belief about the nature of Man as the truth. While I refer to the good–evil dichotomy as belief and myth (guesses), I must point out that the theological tradition would view it as "revealed truth." Later, I will attempt to clarify this apparent difference.

For now it is sufficient to note that the belief of the good-evil dichotomy of Man is deeply entrenched in our current view of the nature of Man, and that this view has been incorporated into psychoanalytic thinking and theory. A single quote from Erik Erikson's *Childhood and Society* is offered here to illuminate this point.

> But the fact remains that the human being in early childhood learns to consider one or the other aspect of bodily function as evil, shameful, or unsafe. There is no culture which does not use a combination of these devils to develop, by way of counterpoint, its own style of faith, pride, certainty, and initiative. Thus there remains in man's sense of achievement the suspicion of its infantile roots; and since his earliest sense of reality was learned by the painful testing of inner and outer goodness and badness, man remains ready to expect from some enemy, force, or event in the outer world that which, in fact, endangers him from

---

7. Alan Richardson, *Christian Apologetics* (New York: Harper & Brothers, 1947), p. 76.

within: from his own angry drives, from his own sense of smallness, and from his split inner world. Thus he is always irrationally ready to fear invasion by vast and vague forces which are other than himself; strangling encirclement by everything that is not safely clarified as allied; and devastating loss of face before all-surrounding, mocking audiences. These, not the animal's fears, characterize human anxiety, and this in world affairs as well as in personal affairs.[8]

Not only has the view of the good-evil dichotomy been incorporated into psychoanalytic theory generally, it has also been incorporated into current psychodynamic theories which, in my view, are the most critical as bases for the understanding of the nature of humanity.

CURRENT PSYCHODYNAMIC THEORY

It is my view that an understanding of the theories of early child development is absolutely essential in obtaining an understanding of the nature of humanity. Any theory of early child development, up to the child's acquisition of language skills, must be based on observation and logical constructs; it is not possible to truly *understand* infants given my previous definition that understanding human beings comes from exploration of language.

What we *know* about infants, as incorporated in current psychodynamic theory, may be briefly sum-

---

8. Erik Erikson, *Childhood and Society* (2d ed.; New York: W.W. Norton & Co., Inc., 1963), p. 406.

marized. Immediately following birth the infant is said to experience a brief period of "normal autism" characterized by an appearance of relative unresponsiveness to external stimuli. Following this brief period, the infant bonds to a mothering figure, which leads to a period of symbiosis or primary narcissism in which the infant appears to experience itself as one with the mothering figure. Beginning at about the fourth or fifth month of life and continuing through the thirtieth to thirty-sixth month, the infant is said to go through an intrapsychic process called separation-individuation. During this period the child also acquires language skills and thus becomes progressively *understandable* rather than merely observable. In the process of separation-individuation, the child becomes progressively aware of its separate existence from its mother (separation) and, coincidentally, progressively aware of its unique, individual characteristics (individuation). This process of separation-individuation has been described by Dr. Margaret Mahler as the psychological birth of the human infant.[9]

The process of separation-individuation provides the basis for understanding the nature of humanity; indeed, any validity of the theory on the nature of humanity herein is contingent on the validity of this process. My understanding of the dynamics of separation-individuation is based primarily on my own un-

---

9. Margaret S. Mahler, Fred Pine, and Anni Bergman, *The Psychological Birth of the Human Infant* (New York: Basic Books, Inc., 1975).

derstanding of the published works of Dr. Margaret Mahler and the published works and teachings of Dr. James Masterson. I will not offer any review of their theories here, but I would commend to the reader a thorough study of their published works. However, *A Theory on the Nature of Humanity,* although based on current psychodynamic theory in general and the work of Mahler and Masterson specifically, offers a significant departure from those theories.

It is my view that the present theoretical interpretation of the end result of separation-individuation is in error. Current theory generally holds that during separation-individuation a defense mechanism may develop called splitting. The result of this defense mechanism is said to allow the child to split internally her or his unacceptable, bad parts from acceptable, good parts. This is seemingly necessary in deference to the aforementioned good-evil dichotomy, and is certainly implicit in the citation from Erikson. It has been the major goal of many therapies, including therapy in my own hands, to rework this split—to integrate the good-bad split self into an integrated whole self. In the section that follows, *A Theory on the Nature of Humanity* will offer a different understanding of the outcome of separation-individuation.

I wish to acknowledge a very specific indebtedness to Dr. Masterson. While attending one of his seminars in New York, I was struck by a statement he made. He simply said that "the therapist's job is to listen and to understand." This dictum was not, of course, peculiar to Dr. Masterson; Freud had made the same or a similar statement years before. I had heard it before. I had *learned* about it during my residency training. But in hearing it from Dr. Masterson that particular day, I *understood* it for the first time. It was, perhaps, the same understanding I was later to come to about Taoism. Exploration through nothingness—that is, exploration in the absence of knowledge and guesses—leads to understanding, to the truth; thus, to listen from nothingness should lead to understanding the person speaking.

II

A THEORY ON THE
NATURE OF HUMANITY

•

HE DISCOVERY OF A THEORY on the nature of humanity occurred primarily in my work as a psycho-therapist. The conditions of therapy, the phenomena observed in therapy, and the results of therapy had been, in my experience, markedly similar to those reported by other psychotherapists who, as I did, based their therapeutic approach on psychoanalytic and psycho-dynamic theories. Patients came on their own accord to examine their emotional despair and, after many hours of difficult work on the part of both patient and therapist, many patients were able to leave therapy with an enhanced sense of self-esteem and self-confi-dence. As noted in the last chapter, a long-standing criticism of the psychotherapeutic process is that it is not scientific, which includes the observation that results of therapy are neither predictable nor reproduc-ible. This correct critical observation has been a proper and serious concern of most psychotherapists, myself included.

Through my own experience as a therapist, I came to a specific understanding that was consistent with the general criticism of our field: I came to recognize that no matter the duration of therapy or the perceived quality of outcome, I ended the process knowing much about the patient but never, in my mind, truly understanding the patient. This led to a time, not precisely known to me, when my liberal arts training allowed me, or perhaps demanded of me, that I begin to explore the observed phenomena in a scholarly, scientific manner; namely, without prejudice. That this began sometime following my hearing Dr. Masterson's reminder "to listen and to understand" seems certain.

In this light a common characteristic of my patients became obvious to me. They were all reasonable. They had all come to therapy as a function of reasonableness—namely, their awareness of their own despair and their desire to do something about it. None of my patients was deprived of reason by the presence of psychosis, dementia, or delerium.

Once this common factor was evident to me I began, with each patient, to ask myself a question taken from British common law as applied to tort cases—namely, "Given these facts and circumstances, what would a reasonable person do?" Why I came to pose this particular question is known only to the perversities of my own mind. The answer to the question was, in every case, the same; given the immediate facts and circumstances of the therapy hour, my patients did not experience or express themselves in a manner that was either reasonable or understandable. I was faced with a paradox: my patients' common factor of reasonableness that had led them to choosing to engage in therapy in the first place versus their observed unreasonableness in response to the facts and circumstances of the therapy hour. From this came a new awareness that there must be something regarding the facts and circumstances of therapy that I did not understand.

Examination of this issue over time led to the discovery of a principle that eventually allowed a new focus for exploration. The principle might be called "the human instinct for self-preservation as seen on a time continuum." In the consulting room it became known to me simply as "the swarm of bees principle," which may be stated as follows: If a reasonable person encounters a swarm of bees (the facts and circumstances of the case), he or she would experience apprehension or fear and would act to avoid the bees. This is understandable in that most people would be expected to have experienced bees in the past and would thus understand that bees are potentially dangerous. In the therapy hour my reasonable patients consistently described themselves as if they were facing a real and immediate danger—the swarm of bees.

At this point I asked myself what was to be a most crucial question. Is it possible to fear and to act to avoid an *historic* swarm of bees? The answer seemed obvious. The historic swarm of bees was the source of the understanding of the dangerousness of bees, but it is unreasonable to fear and impossible to flee *historic* bees. For purposes of further exploration this understanding allowed me, for the moment, to ignore previous psychoanalytic theory and thus to get closer to nothingness.

Since the swarm of bees is not real and present in the therapy room, and since an historic swarm of bees cannot be experienced, then what remains is the future swarm of bees. This led to the conjecture that all of my patients were anticipating a threatening event in the future. I further generally understood that, despite varying styles and varying symptomatic presentations, each of my patients anticipated the same general future event. Some swarm of bees commonly experienced in the past and commonly anticipated in the future had produced a present sense of apprehension or dread.

Surely my patients were not consciously aware of the nature of the swarm of bees or they would have simply told me what it was. Thus it was my responsibility to explore for the answer. This became my focused task for some time, but to no avail. The answer would not be forthcoming until I had made yet another discovery, a discovery that would not only lead to the swarm of bees but would also form the basis for *A Theory on the Nature of Humanity*. What I discovered has always been open for us to understand and experience and is definite in precise, measurable terms. That such discovery has not occurred previously may be explained, in part, by our prejudicial application of theories from the liberal arts and from psychoanalytic schools.

As I posed questions to my patients to explore further what they had revealed of themselves, I chanced one day upon a question to which I got a surprising response. I continued to pose the same question to other patients, and their responses were similar to the response of the first patient. This was even more surprising and not immediately understandable to me. This question, which was eventually to lead to the identity of the swarm of bees, was, "What is it like for you to be embarrassed?"

The eventual discovery of the swarm's identity was delayed yet further, however, because something was still in the way. The barrier, as usual, was that I was holding onto knowledge, holding onto my prejudicial belief in current psychodynamic theory regarding the outcome of the process of separation-individuation and the concept of splitting as a defense mechanism. I was not yet exploring from nothingness. The nothingness came when I allowed myself to ignore these learned concepts. Once I was able to do this, to get even closer to nothingness, I was able to see my patients, indeed human beings in general, in a whole new and illuminating light. Although I had not yet found the swarm of bees at this point, I had found something far more basic. I could now understand that the process of separation-individuation *did not* and *could not* end in a good-bad split self, and that there was no basis for the concept of a splitting defense mechanism.

On the basis of the discovery process described above, it is now my view that the process of separation-individuation results naturally and normally in the creation of two selves that are distinct and different and that are coexistent. I have chosen to call these two selves the Who-Self and the What-Self, and it is the differentiation of the Who-Self from the What-Self that provides the basis for a theory on the nature of humanity.

LINGUISTIC DISTINCTION

A person is the sum total of the Who-Self and What-Self; thus "myself" = Who-Self + What-Self. The Who-Self may be stated as "I am me," *me* being the personal object of *I*; the What-Self may be stated as "I am a what," *what* being the impersonal object of *I*.

DEVELOPMENTAL DISTINCTION

The theory described in chapter one of the intrapsychic process of separation-individuation that leads to the psychological birth of the infant remains valid; if that theory should be eventually disproven, then this theory will likewise be disproven. However, a theory on the nature of humanity holds that the process of individuation leads to the development of the Who-Self, while the process of separation leads to the development of the What-Self. The process of separa-

tion-individuation is now seen as two separate processes that occur simultaneously, in concert, leading
to the development of two separate entities, the Who-
Self and the What-Self. Splitting, therefore, is a natural
part of development and not a defense mechanism.

GENERAL CHARACTERISTICS

The Who-Self is comprised of one's unique perceptions of the world around herself or himself and of
one's values, tastes, emotions, desires, fantasies, imagination and impulses, and, finally, one's awareness of
the human characteristic of fallibility. During the
process of individuation, the child becomes increasingly aware of the individual, unique characteristics
of the Who-Self and, concomitantly, becomes increasingly aware that its Who-Self is distinctly different
from every other Who-Self in the world. At the end
of the process of individuation, at about age three,
the child's Who-Self is complete, and the child is aware
of its uniqueness.[1]

The What-Self is comprised of all of the genetically
determined, species-specific features of *Homo sapiens*
including gender and ethnicity; it is further comprised
of language, nationality, intellect (including reason,
logic, and capacity for directed thought), and occupation (including any activities requiring intellectual,
language, or motor skills). During the process of sep-

---

1. This may not hold true for identical twins. See the heading "Identical
Twins" in the next chapter.

aration the child becomes increasingly aware of its existence as a separate being—as being separate from its mother, as being the child of a specific set of parents, as being of the human species, as being male or female, as being one of a specific ethnic group, and as being capable of learning language and motor skills.

IDENTITY

One derives a personal identity by way of one's awareness of the Who-Self, which is distinct from all other Who-Selves. In contrast, one derives an impersonal identity from awareness of the What-Self, which is similar to other What-Selves. In our present culture there has been an expressed interest in and concern for something called an "indentity crisis." Such crises and confusion based in identity do indeed occur, and these may now be understood as a confusion between the Who-Self and the What-Self. The issue of indentity confusion will be further explored in chapter three, the commentary section.

CHOICE AND WILL

The Who-Self is not a choice. At any given moment one's tastes, one's values, one's unique perceptions of the world, one's desires, fastasies, imaginations, impulses, emotions, and human fallibility are absolute. One cannot choose or will them to be different. In awareness of the dynamic human capacity for human growth we understand that the Who-Self can and surely will change over time, and that choices can be made to encourage and nurture that growth, but at time present the Who-Self is absolute, it is not a choice. For example, what I desire for myself today and what I hold of personal value today are different from that which I desired for myself or held as valuable twenty years ago, but the change came from a process of growth and maturation; it did not occur by choice or will. With regard to emotions, if one is aware of feeling sad or angry or joyous, then for that moment the emotion is absolute; one cannot choose or will a different emotion. Whatever part of the Who-Self one is aware of is absolute for the moment.

The What-Self, with two exceptions, is always a choice. The exceptions are (1) being human, being a *Homo sapiens*, and (2) being the child of a specific set of parents. We cannot choose to be of a different species and we cannot choose a different set of biological (genetic) parents. These two exceptions of the What-Self as a choice, when viewed in the context of the Who-Self What-Self dichotomy, raise fascinating theoretical questions for philosophy and theology, questions that will be addressed in the commentary section. All other aspects of the What-Self, of impersonal indentity, are subject to choice and will, including language spoken, residence, occupation, nonoccupational activities, subjects to learn, membership in organizations, and mate.

EXAMPLE: If one should desire to become a blacksmith, then the desire, which belongs to the Who-Self, may be acted upon and the person may apprentice him/herself to a master blacksmith. The person is then a blacksmith What-Self, a What-Self that has been chosen. Moreover, at any time this person can choose to stop being a blacksmith. In this example, the What-Self is a choice to be in or out of an occupation.

EXPRESSION VERSUS EXPLANATION

The Who-Self can be expressed with language. If the expression is in clear, precise language, then the Who-Self is understandable. The Who-Self cannot be explained, it can only be expressed. In contrast, the What-Self can be explained, but cannot be expressed.

EXAMPLE: I can express to you my personal Who-Self love for the coast of Maine and my desire to live there someday, but I cannot explain that to you, I cannot justify it with logic or reason; it is merely a part of my Who-Self. In contrast, if I were a blacksmith What-Self I would be able to explain that to you, to explain what a blacksmith does, how it is done, why something is done one way and not another, and what one needs to learn to become a blacksmith. I could not express blacksmithing to you; I could only express to you what it is like for me personally, as a Who-Self, to be a blacksmith. I could, however, explain to you how to be a blacksmith. I cannot explain to you how to be a James Thomas.

MEASURABILITY

The Who-Self is singular and unique. No Who-Self can have exactly the same tastes, values, perceptions, desires, fantasies, impulses, or emotions as another Who-Self. And, since the Who-Self is singular, the Who-Self cannot be measured; you cannot measure 1. Therefore, the Who-Self cannot be good or bad, cannot be criticized, and cannot be discriminated.

The What-Self, in contrast, is one of many and common. Therefore, the What-Self is measurable. The What-Self may be seen as better or worse than other What-Selves, can be criticized, and can be discriminated. In measuring a specific What-Self, the standards of measurement must be explicit, fair, and uniformly applied in order for the measurement to be valid.

EXAMPLE: As a blacksmith What-Self I can be measured in comparison with other blacksmiths; I can be *relatively* good or bad. As a blacksmith What-Self I can be criticized because of my measurability, and if I want to be a successful blacksmith that criticism is important to me. When I have finished a piece of work, the master blacksmith may say, "That is not good enough, do it over" or "That is a masterful piece of work." Either criticism is equally valuable to me. Finally, as a function of my What-Self measurability I am properly open to discrimination. The master blacksmith, my blacksmith peers, and the customers of my trade may and will measure my skills and discriminate me as better or worse than other blacksmiths. But my Who-Self, which coexists with my blacksmith What-Self, cannot be measured, criticized or discriminated.

EXAMPLE: In the story of Goldilocks and the three bears, Goldilocks, through exploration, discovers that "Papa Bear's porridge is too hot, Mama Bear's porridge is too cold, and Baby Bear's porridge is just right." This is an expression of Goldilock's Who-Self indicating her own unique perceptions and her individual values and tastes; these cannot be generalized to any other Who-Selves. Goldilock's discovery does not tell us anything about the porridge other than the probability that Papa Bear's porridge is relatively warmer than and Mama Bear's porridge is relatively cooler than Baby Bear's porridge. Her statement does not provide an explicit measurement of the porridge; the temperature of the porridge remains unknown. The three bowls of porridge are analogous to What-Selves, such as three blacksmiths, and the porridge can be measured and discriminated on the basis of temperature, texture, volume, taste, and color.

EQUALITY

In that the Who-Self is singular, unique, and not amenable to measurement, it follows that one's Who-Self is equal to all other Who-Selves. Here I would note that mathematicians would properly insist on the term *noncomparable* rather than *equal,* but the fact remains that one's Who-Self cannot be better or worse than another's Who-Self. Thus one's perceptions, values, tastes, desires, emotions, fantasies, and impulses cannot be good or bad. There is no good-evil dichotomy in the Who-Self. If one *acts* on an emotion or impulse, it is as a What-Self (blacksmith, parent, citizen, etc.) that she or he acts, and the What-Self is measurable.

The What-Self is one of many, is common, and is amenable to measurement, and thus the What-Self is, by definition, always unequal. Or, in mathematical language, What-Selves are comparable and therefore unequal. No two blacksmiths can have precisely the same skills, and their skills can be measured against some set of standards. Since being a What-Self is a choice, and since What-Selves are unequal and relatively good or bad, then being relatively good or bad is a choice. This again argues against the existence of a good-evil dichotomy intrinsic to humans.

SIMILARITY

The Who-Self in its unmeasurable uniqueness is always dissimilar from all other Who-Selves. Who-Selves are always dissimilar and equal.

The What-Self in its measurable commonness is always similar to other What-Selves; a blacksmith What-Self is similar to all other blacksmiths in the world. What-Selves are always similar and unequal.

HIERARCHY

Since Who-Selves are dissimilar and equal they cannot be placed in any hierarchy. As a Who-Self one cannot be higher or lower, better or worse, bigger or smaller than any other Who-Self in the world.

Since What-Selves are similar and unequal they fall naturally into hierarchies. These hierarchies may or may not be formally organized, but any specific What-Self is, as a function of measurability, higher or lower, better or worse than other What-Selves.

NATURAL VERSUS ACQUIRED SKILLS

Another distinction between the Who-Self and the What-Self may be seen in the distinction between natural and acquired skills. The Who-Self has all of its necessary skills available early in life. The choice of each new and different What-Self demands the acquisition of a new, specific set of learned skills.

The Who-Self possesses the natural, innate skill of being aware of its own emotions, impulses, desires, fantasies, values, and tastes. Through its natural, innate sensory skills of sight, hearing, taste, touch, and smell, it is capable of being aware of the world immediately around itself. These awareness and sensory skills do not have to be learned and are available to the Who-Self at the earliest stages of development.

The What-Self, in contrast, must acquire skills through learning in order to be successful, and each specific What-Self requires a specific set of skills.

These acquired, learned skills fall into one of three categories: (1) intellectual skills, (2) language skills, and (3) motor skills. These skills are acquired over time and are *not* available at the earliest stages of development.

EXPLORATION VERSUS LEARNING

The Who–Self, using its natural skills of awareness, is able to explore its own Who–Self and to explore the external world. Such exploration leads to understanding, truth, wisdom, and maturity. Such exploration does not require any specific intellectual, language, or motor skills. The wisdom of the Who–Self can only be understood by others through expression with language, but the wisdom derived from exploration does not have to be expressed by the Who–Self or understood by others in order to be valid. The Who–Self does not need to be validated by others, and, in fact, it cannot be validated or invalidated by others. Therefore, acquired language skills are not necessary to achieve individual Who–Self understanding, truth, wisdom, and maturity. This view is similar to and consistent with the view of Taoism, which states that the path to wisdom is to explore from nothingness. That small children can and do possess understanding and wisdom will be considered below under "Essence and Existence."

The What–Self must learn intellectual, language, and motor skills to be a specific What–Self, and this learning leads to knowledge. The successful blacksmith has a specific set of knowledge and *knows* about blacksmithing; a citizen of Denmark has a set of knowledge, including knowledge of the Danish language, and *knows* about being Danish; a tennis player has a set of knowledge about tennis, including acquired (learned) motor skills, and *knows* about tennis. In all cases, the knowledge arrived at through learning meets the definition of the What-Self in being a choice, in being explainable, and in being measurable.

The maxim of Taoism that "the learned are not wise and the wise are not learned" can now be stated in different terms as follows: The What-Self (learned) is not a Who-Self (wise) and the Who-Self (wise) is not a What-Self (learned). The Who-Self, with its natural skills, achieves wisdom through exploration, whereas the What-Self, with its acquired skills, achieves knowledge through learning.

RESPONSIVE VERSUS RESPONSIBLE

The Who-Self, in being aware of itself and the world around it, can be responsive, can answer to itself. Whether the response is to an awareness of an emotion or to the world around, it is a response made back to the Who-Self.

The What-Self is responsible and must answer to others. The blacksmith is responsible for the choice of becoming a blacksmith, is responsible for being able to explain blacksmithing, and is responsible to the measurements that apply to blacksmithing.

Both the Who-Self and the What-Self can respond

(answer), but the Who-Self is responsive to its own awareness, whereas the What-Self is responsible to (must answer to) standards of measurement. Thus, the Who-Self is responsive but not responsible, and the What-Self is responsible and not responsive.

INDEPENDENT VERSUS DEPENDENT

A corollary to the distinction between the responsiveness of the Who-Self and the responsibility of the What-Self allows a distinction between independence and dependence. The Who-Self, in its nonchoice, nonexplainable, nonmeasurable awareness, is independent and free and in this independence and freedom may explore for understanding, truth, wisdom, and maturity.

The What-Self, in its state of choice, explainability, and measurability, is dependent and restricted. In choosing a specific What-Self for itself, the What-Self is restricted by what must be learned and known and by what is being measured.

EXPOSURE

One more feature of the Who-Self What-Self dichotomy requires understanding before returning to the search for the swarm of bees. We have a wide range of freedom as to when, where, and to whom we expose what we are—the What-Self—and an even wider range of freedom as to when, where, and to whom we expose who we are—the Who-Self. If I were walking along a beach where others were sun-

ning or swimming or playing, I would be an undif-
ferentiated person to the casual observer. All that
would be seen would be my identity as a human being,
the nonchoice What-Self *Homo sapiens.* I could choose
to spend the entire day at the beach without exposing
who I am or what I am. However, if there were an
accident on the beach and someone shouted out, "Is
anyone a doctor here?" I would feel a moral and ethical
obligation to identify myself as a physician, to expose
a What-Self. I could then, as a What-Self physician,
offer medical treatment to a What-Self patient, but
during that time it would not be necessary for me to
express and expose my Who-Self or to reveal any of
my other What-Selves. At the end of the emergency
I could continue my walk along the beach now dif-
ferentiated to observers as a physician What-Self. My
Who-Self could remain unexpressed and unexposed,
and my other What-Selves could remain unexposed.
This freedom to choose when and where and to whom
we reveal our identity, including the freedom to reveal
the Who-Self or the What-Self and not both, allows
us the choice of conducting our public lives as one or
another What-Self while our Who-Self remains unexposed and private.

EMBARRASSMENT AND HUMILIATION
(THE SWARM OF BEES)

And now back to the exploration. Once the distinction between the Who-Self and the What-Self became
evident and once this distinction began to be under-

stood in the consulting room, a whole new avenue
of exploration became available. I now return to the
issue of embarrassment, which is the exclusive property of the Who-Self.

It is a characteristic of human beings that they are
fallible. We are capable of making err★rs, of being
inaccurate, of being misled, of being duped, and of
being fooled. Conscious awareness of our fallibility
leads to a natural state of anxiety and discomfort.
Anxiety and discomfort are experienced in anticipation of the expression and exposure of our fallibility,
which leads to embarrassment. We may also express
and expose our fallibility without prior conscious
awareness, which also leads to embarrassment, but
without the anticipatory anxiety and discomfort.
Since the experience of embarrassment belongs to the
Who-Self it can be experienced in the absence of
others. Most of us have experienced private embarrassing moments. The experience of embarrassment,
with or without anticipatory anxiety, is an expression
of our humanness. Embarrassment leads to humor
and laughter, which celebrate our humanity. The innate human characteristic of fallibility puts us constantly at risk of embarrassment; we cannot protect
ourselves from it. We human beings are, after all,
very funny creatures.

The connection between embarrassment and humor
has been well documented by others and will only be
touched on briefly here. Laughter is an expression of
embarrassment; that is to say, we laugh in response

to experiencing embarrassment. We laugh not so much at the content of a joke, but at the punch line, which catches us off guard. It is not what we had expected; we recognize that we have been misled, been duped, and we experience embarrassment and laugh. Thus, laughter is absent the second time we hear the joke, because we can no longer be caught off guard. When we are aware of others making errors or being fooled, we are reminded of our own innate fallibility, we resonate with the other's embarrassment, and we laugh. This is the basis for humor in the theater, literature, the movies, television, and in social encounters.

I will now describe a specific example of embarrassment and will refer to it later in contrast. A woman visits a city unfamiliar to her and stays in a motel; there is no basis for embarrassment if she sits beside the motel swimming pool attired in a two-piece bathing suit. Later, back in her motel room, she has a shower, puts on bra and panties, and stands in front of a mirror brushing her hair. A bell boy taking new guests to their room mistakenly opens the door to the room where the woman is standing. Everyone has been caught off guard, everyone is surprised, everyone experiences embarrassment leading to blushing, stammered apologies, and awkward retreats. If we were to see this scene portrayed on television or in a movie, we would identify and resonate with the embarrassment, and we would laugh.

Despite this relationship between embarrassment and laughter, my patients, when asked, "What is it like for you to be embarrassed?" consistently gave no evidence of humor or laughter in their responses. Instead, their responses expressed varying degrees of despair, rage, helplessness, hopelessness, loss of dignity, emptiness, impulses to flee or to cower, and an impulse to get revenge. I recognized these as predictable and natural responses to experiences of humiliation but **not** as natural responses to embarrassment.

Humiliation always comes from the hands of others who have some power, authority, or advantage that they misuse to force us to do something or to experience something that we would not naturally choose to do or to experience. Since humiliation is dependent on the presence of power, authority, or advantage, it can only occur in a relationship with a What-Self because it is the unequalness of What-Selves that provides the basis for power, authority, and advantage. Humiliation is always unnatural and is always destructive to human dignity, destructive to the integrity of the Who-Self. As What-Selves we are always unequal, and there will always be somebody or somebodies who have power, advantage, or authority. Therefore, as What-Selves, we are always at risk of humiliation.

Let us go back for a moment to the story of the woman in the motel. If, while she is standing brushing her hair, the phone rings and the caller states, "We have your children captive and if you ever want to

see them again you will have to do what I say; I want
you to go outside in your bra and panties and then
walk the length of the city down Main Street," then
the woman is the object of humiliation. Despite the
fact that walking down a city street in bra and panties
is not significantly more revealing than sitting at pool-
side in a bikini, she is now being forced to do something that is unnatural and destructive to human dignity. If, in contrast, she were to step out onto the
balcony of her motel while attired in her lingerie and
the wind blew the door shut and it locked, that would
be embarrassing but not humiliating.

It is, of course, possible for embarrassment to be
turned into humiliation, but only by another person
or persons who have some power or authority or
advantage. If I were presenting a public lecture and I
made a glaring error or I discovered that I had brought
the wrong prepared text or that my fly was open, I
might experience embarrassment. I could acknowledge my embarrassment and laugh at myself, and my
audience could share in the laughter, could share in
the celebration of my humanness. If, however, the
audience laughed at me or jeered me derisively, then
the embarrassment could be turned into an experience
of humiliation.

Another illustration taken from my own experiences may further illuminate the point. As a young
boy I reacted with abject abhorrence to the films of
atrocities during World War II in Europe and in Asia.
I continue to react to these scenes and to memories

of these scenes with abhorrence, the intensity of which has not diminished over the years. What I was reacting to was not the scenes of people dying; death is a natural part of life. What I was reacting to, and continue to react to, are the scenes of human beings being publicly humiliated, being forced to do things that are unnatural. That is as much a threat to my human dignity as it was to theirs.

It is now my understanding that the experience of humiliation is the anticipated swarm of bees. It is in anticipation of humiliation, based on experiences of humiliation in the past—the historic swarm of bees— that despair is experienced in the present. The experience of humiliation is the basis for all human fear. Stated formally, the principle of a theory on the nature of humanity is:

> **All psychological defenses are
> developed to protect against
> humiliation and humiliation alone.**

It follows that all defense mechanisms observed in the therapy hour, or anywhere else for that matter, indicate anticipation of humiliation in the future. Since psychological defense mechanisms appear to be ubiquitous among human beings (they are not the unique property of patients in psychotherapy), the fear of humiliation can be called a basic human fear.

The person as Who-Self in awareness of its human fallibility, with or without public exposure, may experience embarrassment, which, in turn, leads to humor and laughter in celebration of our humanness. Embarrassment is natural. The person as What-Self is always at the risk of humiliation in that in the hierarchy of What-Selves someone with power, authority, or advantage may misuse that power to force him or her to do or to experience something that is unnatural. The experience of humiliation is a threat to our human dignity.

The distinction between embarrassment as a natural function of the Who-Self and humiliation as an unnatural function of the What-Self now seems evident and is applicable to all human beings. It would follow that any human being having experienced humiliation in the past—the historic swarm of bees—would understandably be wary of future experiences of humiliation —the anticipated swarm of bees. The unreasonable character of my patients in the therapy hour, which was discussed previously, is based on what appears to be an unrealistic anticipation of humiliation, as if humiliation were going to occur in the next instant. This unrealistic anticipation is further compounded by my patients' seeming inability to distinguish between embarrassment and humiliation and, in fact, between their Who-Selves and their What-Selves. Furthermore, in the very recent past, I have become increasingly aware of the fact that, in my patients, there appears to be a direct correlation between the variety and intensity of psychological defenses in the present with the quantity of historical humiliating experiences in the past. It is my view that my patients are no different from all other human beings except in their historical experiences with humiliation. They are not sick or abnormal.

It is my view that many human conditions currently described as psychopathological may now be understood on the basis of the recognition that some persons lack the ability to distinguish between the Who-Self and the What-Self and, therefore, lack the ability to distinguish the difference between embarrassment and humiliation. Since human beings are aware that we cannot protect ourselves against experiences of embarrassment, then these persons experience themselves as unable to be protected from humiliation. How this affects the definition of psychopathology will be addressed in chapter three.

ESSENCE VERSUS EXISTENCE
(SOLITUDE AND INTIMACY VERSUS SURVIVAL)

There is a long-standing philosophical and theological question concerning the distinction between essence and existence. This issue will be explored more fully in the commentaries of the next chapter. At this point, I will simply offer the proposition that essence may be seen as being the Who-Self, and existence may be seen as a function of the What-Self. To state this yet another way, the Who-Self may be seen as essential for essence or living, while the What-Self may be seen as essential for existence or surviving.

Given the present structure of Western civilization, one needs to be a good enough What–Self to survive. Our society's preoccupation with success attests to this fact. Even when people are not very successful and cannot find employment, they have to be good enough as welfare recipients (What–Selves) in order to survive. The welfare recipient is measured, has to fill out forms, has to be interviewed by a case worker, and must show up in person at regular intervals to receive checks. Therefore, being a What–Self is for survival (existence) and is dependent on acquired survival skills.

What–Selves are always at the risk of two experiences. First, the What–Self may be rejected, may be found unacceptable. This may be experienced as unpleasant, but it is not destructive if it reflects an appropriate use of authority to measure. Second, the What–Self may be humiliated, which is destructive and reflects a *misuse* of authority, power, or advantage.

EXAMPLE: If a student What–Self scores 30 on an examination and receives an F grade, then the student understands that he or she is not good enough. Perhaps this is painful, but it is not destructive because the professor has used his or her authority in a responsible manner. If, however, in passing out the examination papers the professor says, "I commend the class on its hard work and success. You all did very well with the single exception of Dan. Unlike the rest of you, he is a miserible excuse for a student," this is a misuse of authority that leads to humiliation.

Since as What-Selves we are always at the risk of being rejected and humiliated, there can be no freedom or happiness or peace in merely surviving as What-Selves. It is satisfying to be a good enough What-Self so that one can survive, and it is even more satisfying to be successful and to survive well. But no matter how well one might be surviving, the risks of rejection and humiliation are omnipresent. Surviving is merely existing, is merely existence.

In contrast, experiences of the Who-Self are for living, are for the essence of life wherein there is no risk of rejection or humiliation and, as will be seen later, there is an opportunity for freedom, happiness, and peace. Who-Self experiences are for the essence of living and are different from the What-Self experiences of survival. The Who-Self experiences that provide freedom, peace, and happiness are found in solitude and intimacy.

SOLITUDE AND INTIMACY

The experience of solitude is described by people in somewhat differing ways, but the differences are minor. In the context of a theory on the nature of humanity, solitude may be defined as a pure experience of the Who-Self while being oblivious to the What-Self, an experience of the essence of life while detached from the mere existence of life. The following words are frequently used in describing experiences of solitude: quiet, peaceful, serene, tranquil, calm, free, joyous, happy, mindless, refreshing, and rejuvenating. In this state one is free to do or to be aware of anything but does not *have* to do or be aware of anything in particular. Solitude is the state of being aware of the Who-Self and of the sights, sounds, smells, and sensations of the immediate environment while being totally oblivious to all else in the world including the responsibilities of the What-Self. It is being at peace with the Who-Self and with immediate surroundings. It is the awareness of living (essence) and the unawareness of the need to survive (existence). In being oblivious to the What-Self there is no risk of rejection or humiliation, so there is an absence of anxiety, fear, anger, helplessness, hopelessness, and of any aggressive or destructive impulses. It is *only* in solitude that one can have freedom, peace, and happiness; these are not available in the What-Self experiences of survival. Solitude may be seen as the same as the Taoist "way of nothingness."

EXAMPLE: In the Army one is strictly a What-Self and usually isn't permitted to express the Who-Self. Being in this position is quite manageable because the positions of authority and power are exquisitely clear and the measurements of what is good enough are explicit. It is not all that difficult to survive in the Army. If one is on a long march, the regulations (the standards of measurement) state that there is to be a five-minute rest break each hour. If the break isn't given, then the commanding officer isn't good enough and is open to rejection by his superior. When the break does come, it is possible to ex-

perience five minutes of solitude, of being oblivious to the Army and to the rest of the world.
Then one can return to the march refreshed. Even
during the march one can experience moments
of solitude; it is possible to march mindlessly.

Thus, in even the most exacting What-Self situations,
one can have moments of getting to the Who-Self in
solitude and of experiencing freedom, peace, and happiness. Of course, one cannot remain suspended in
solitude indefinitely. Sooner or later one must return
to the What-Self in order to survive.

To re-emphasize: the *only* source of freedom, peace,
and happiness is in solitude. No one can give solitude
to you, and no one can make it happen for you. However, the experience of solitude can be enriched and
enhanced by the presence of another person in intimacy. In order to experience intimacy, people must
be present as pure Who-Selves, oblivious to their own
and others' What-Selves. Or, from another perspective, intimacy is two or more persons experiencing
solitude in concert. The word *intimacy* derives from
the Latin *intimus,* the superlative case of *intus,* which
means *within;* thus, intimacy is being within one's self
(Who-Self) in the company of another. In intimacy
persons may do or be aware of or think or say whatever they wish, but they do not *have* to do or be aware
of or think or say anything in particular. They are
free. They are dissimilar and equal and understand
that all that can be done with their own and others'
Who-Selves is to understand and accept them. In their

equality as unmeasurable Who-Selves, they cannot possess power or authority or advantage, so there is no risk of rejection or humiliation, and there is no basis for anxiety, fear, despair, anger, or impulses of fleeing or cowering or aggression.

Solitude can be rather easily accessible, whereas intimate relationships, as defined here, are rare and precious. In our What-Self world of survival, it is all too uncommon for people to take time for intimacy, even though most people express a desire for intimacy. It seems probable that many persons experience a type of intimacy with pets or domestic farm animals. It would seem true that such experiences with animals cannot enrich or enhance solitude to the same degree as human intimacy but, nonetheless, the presence of a specific animal may enrich one's solitude.

Because a child is free of responsibility for survival (thanks to undeveloped What-Self survival skills and the availability of parents' What-Self skills), she or he is marvelously free to experience solitude and, in that solitude, to explore actively the immediate environment—all of the sights, sounds, smells, tastes, and sensations available. At this time, exploration, no matter how active, is peaceful, free, happy, and mindless. Children engage in whatever strikes their fancy and do not *have* to do anything in particular. This, no doubt, is the basis for adults often describing the experience of solitude as rejuvenating. This also explains, for me, the boundless joy of watching children. There is nothing more to say about the child's Who-

Self. As with any Who-Self, all that you can do with it is to understand it and accept it. It is also permissible, in my view, to marvel at the child's Who-Self.

Children are often described as being innocent. Innocence might be defined as the state of having access to the Who-Self and exploring the immediate world around oneself while being oblivious to the What-Self world of survival and existence because someone else, namely a parent, has responsibility for that. Innocence is similar to the adult experience of solitude, but adults arrive at solitude *from* a state of surviving and understand that eventually they will need to return to the What-Self world. As adults, we understand that no one is taking care of us, that we have to do that for ourselves.

I once *learned* that "the price of wisdom is innocence," that we have to divest ourselves of innocence in order to be wise. That made sense at the time, but now I understand that the price of knowledge is innocence. It is possible to be both innocent and wise. Children are innocent and, although their world is very small, within its perimeter they are infinitely wise. I would offer the view that, even for adults, it is preferable to be wise about a small world than to be merely knowledgeable about a larger world.

In summary, the Who-Self experiences of solitude and intimacy and the experience of innocence in childhood provide the essence of life, with such experiences leading to understanding, truth, wisdom, and maturity. These Who-Self experiences rely on the natural,

innate skills of awareness of self and sensory perceptions of the environment. The What-Self experiences
of success provide survival for existence, but all such
experiences put one at the risk of rejection and humiliation. These experiences rely on learned intellectual,
language, and motor skills. As What-Self I am responsible for my existence; as Who-Self I am responsive
to my essence.

BEING VERSUS DOING

Being who you are, the Who-Self, just is; doing
what you do, the What-Self, is reasoned.

As a What-Self, including a What-Self member of
society, we are expected to conduct ourselves—to
do—in a reasonable, orderly, timely fashion. Our
What-Self action may be measured as reasonable or
unreasonable, logical or illogical, orderly, or disorderly as implied in the question from British common
law, "Given these facts and circumstances, what
would a reasonable person *do*?" The question is not
what would a reasonable person *feel* or what would
a reasonable person *want* to do.

The Who-Self, in being, just is and is not amenable
to reason or logic. The intellectual function of the
human mind is part of What-Self skills and is analogous to a computer in that it is logical and dispassionate.
Human intellect is also analogous to the computer in
that the mind can be programmed, logically, with
utter nonsense. A dictum of computer technology is
"garbage in, garbage out." Learning, however reason-

able and logical, only leads to knowledge, but not to understanding or wisdom.

If one has the desire to go fishing and the impulse to take the day off from work to do so, this is an awareness of the Who-Self and just is. The desire and the impulse are neither reasonable nor unreasonable, logical or illogical, orderly or disorderly; they just are. To act on this desire and impulse, to go fishing and to not go to work, are reasoned acts; thus, the doing may be measured as reasonable or unreasonable. The Who-Self in being may be understood, while the What-Self in doing may be known, and may be known as reasonable or unreasonable. The Who-Self in solitude or in intimacy may act freely and the doing need not be reasoned.

VALUES VERSUS
ETHICS AND MORALS

Values belong to the Who-Self and are, thus, not a choice, not explainable, and not measurable. One's values may be dissimilar from the values of other Who-Selves, but they are always equal to them. Values can be expressed, but they cannot be explained. Values are not hierarchical.

Ethics and morals are standards of measurement for What-Selves as members of a specific society. By these standards, What-Selves are deemed as acceptable members of the society (good enough) or they are deemed as unacceptable members of the society (not good enough). Ethics and morals are chosen, are explainable, and are standards of measurement. A society's code of laws usually stands as an explicit statement of that society's ethics and morals. They apply to what people *do* as What-Selves; they do not apply to the Who-Selves. One's perceptions, tastes, values, emotions, fantasies, desires, and impulses cannot be measured by ethics and morals. The Who-Self cannot be unethical or immoral.

SEPARATE AND/OR TOGETHER

As a What-Self one may be either separate *or* together. For example, the What-Self of a student at the university is together with the university, is part of the university. This togetherness does not change when the student is away on holiday; the student is still part of the university. If the student chooses to stop being a student or if, in being measured, the student is found to be not good enough and is failed from the university (rejected), then he or she is separate from the university and no longer together with the university. Thus, a What-Self is either separate *or* together.

As a Who-Self, in personal Who-Self relationships, one is always separate *and* together. Since one's Who-Self is unique and singular, and since one can only be aware of one's own Who-Self, the Who-Self is always separate. The Who-Self is always together with all other Who-Selves in the shared condition of humanness. Thus, the Who-Self is always separate *and* together.

What-Self relationships, in being separate *or* together, stand in distinct contrast to Who-Self relationships, which are separate *and* together. As noted earlier, intimacy requires the exclusion of What-Selves. Thus, intimate relationships are separate *and* together. It is a matter of common observation that, in seeking intimacy, many people attempt to be together but not separate, which will not lead to intimacy. Shel Silverstein portrays this distinction in his book *The Missing Piece Meets the Big O* in a manner that is as marvelous as it is simple.[2] The Missing Piece, who keeps searching for another so that they can be together and not separate (What-Selves), eventually finds the Big O and discovers that it is possible to be separate and together (Who-Selves).

THE HUMAN DILEMMA

In order to survive, one must be successful as a What-Self, and the What-Self is always at the risk of humiliation. It is the experience of humiliation that leads to the ultimate human dilemma. The final statement of a theory on the nature of humanity addresses this human dilemma.

In distinct contrast to many philosophical, theological, and humanitarian views, it is my view that it is natural for human beings to experience rage and an impulse for revenge in response to the experience of

---

2. Shel Silverstein, *The Missing Piece Meets the Big O* (New York: Harper & Rowe, 1981).

humiliation. In fact, as a member of human society, that is, as a *nonchoice* What-Self, the impulse for revenge may be understood as a desire to retaliate in defense of collective human dignity and not simply in response to personal harm. Even if the rage and impulse for revenge are accepted as natural and human, as they must be in my view, one is faced with the choice of acting on the impulse, which would lead to humiliating the humiliator. I have described humiliation as being unnatural and destructive to human dignity; therefore, for one who values human dignity the act of humiliating another would be intolerable. This intolerable state I will define with the word *shame*. For purposes of this discussion, the word *shame* is restricted to the definition of the state of one who misuses authority, power, or advantage to humiliate another. Thus the dilemma: if one is humiliated, one responds naturally with rage and an impulse for revenge; but to act on this impulse leads to shame. Since thé act of humiliation is a destructive act against human dignity, the resultant shame cannot be forgiven by the person humiliated; that forgiveness can only come from the collected human dignity, from the whole of humanity.

This, then, is the ultimate human dilemma: In response to being humiliated, one may feel helpless, hopeless, a loss of dignity, emptiness, rage, impulses to flee or to cower, and an impulse for revenge. These may be seen collectively as a description of ultimate human despair. The impulses available are to flee or

cower, neither of which offers relief from the humiliation, or to get revenge, which, if acted upon, leads
to shame. Thus, the choice appears to be between
tolerating the despair and loss of human dignity or
having shame. It is my view that this dilemma, which
results from any experience of humiliation, provides
a basis for understanding all human despair. A more
complete description of this dilemma and a resolution
of the dilemma are offered in the next chapter.

SUMMARY

Myself = Who-self + What-self

Who-Self	*What-Self*
1. I am me: me as personal object of I	I am a what: what as impersonal object of I
2. Develops from individuation	Develops from separation
3. Personal identity	Impersonal identity
4. Nonchoice	Choice
5. Can be expressed but not explained	Can be explained but not expressed
6. Not measurable	Measurable
7. Equal	Unequal
8. Dissimilar	Similar
9. Not hierarchical	Hierarchical
10. Natural skills	Acquired skills
11. Responsive	Responsible
12. Independent	Dependent
13. Embarrassment	Humiliation
14. Essence	Existence
15. Exploring	Learning
16. Being	Doing
17. Values	Ethics and morals
18. Separate *and* together	Separate *or* together

III

COMMENTARY

INCE HUMAN NATURE AND the Who-Self can only be understood through experience and language, the human dilemma must be presented in a descriptive rather than a prescriptive manner. I will now attempt to describe the dilemma so that the reader may understand it on the basis of his or her own experiences.

THE DILEMMA REVISITED

Most, if not all people, have had the experience of having a full bladder to the point of discomfort or even pain, but such an experience is not frightening because one understands that relief is eventually available.

The experience of a full bladder is analogous to the experience of the Who-Self; no one can see your bladder, touch your bladder, be aware of your bladder, or make statements about your bladder. It would be nonsensical for someone to tell you to go to the bathroom because they felt that your bladder was full. Likewise, if you were to state your need to go to the bathroom for relief, the following responses would also be nonsensical: "That's dumb for you to feel that way!" "You couldn't possibly need to go." "My bladder doesn't feel full so I know your's doesn't." "I'll decide when you need to go." As absurd as these statements seem, it is tragically commonplace for people to make statements about another's Who-Self as if the statements were true. For example, the Who-Self expression "I feel angry" is often responded to with statements such as "oh you shouldn't feel that way," or "that's stupid," or "you don't really feel angry," or "it's evil to feel that way." In fact, you are the only one in the world who can be aware of who you are; no one can see your Who-Self, touch your Who-Self, or make statements about your Who-Self. When you express your Who-Self in language, all that another person can do is to understand and accept who you are.

All of the following expressions of the Who-Self are immediately understandable: (1) "My house was struck by lightning last night and burned to the ground. I am overcome with grief, but I'm glad that no one was injured." (2) "Someone ran into my new car and wrecked it, and I'm enraged." (3) "My friends gave me a surprise birthday party last week and I was delighted." (4) "When the window of my study blew open, I was momentarily startled." Such responses to events in our lives are analogous to the full bladder in that we understand that eventually, with time, we will get relief, and thus we are not frightened. No matter how painful or joyous our experiences might be, we can experience them fully without fear because we understand that we will not be *stuck* with these feelings forever, that we will eventually have relief. (I submit that intense, interminable joy would be as uncomfortable and unnatural as intense, interminable sadness.) Relief from feeling startled when the window blows open comes in a matter of seconds, whereas relief from feeling sad when one's house burns may not come for months, but one understands that relief will indeed come, that one will not be stuck in sadness forever.

The following extention of the example of the full bladder is more symbolic than factual, but I believe it will make the point. If one experiences a full bladder and discovers that urination is not possible, then that is cause for concern. Most people know that this does sometimes happen because they have some general knowledge that kidney stones, bladder infections, and muscle spasms may lead to the inability to urinate. We understand that this condition is not mystical or magical. Should the discomfort and inability to urinate persist, then one might seek medical consultation for relief. If then the physician, after conducting what seems to be a thorough examination, says, "There is nothing that can be done for you," one might, after a moment of disbelief, have increased concern or fear and a desire to seek a second opinion. For purposes of this discussion, let it be given that there is no relief available, that the bladder is full to the point of being painful, that urination is not possible, and that medical science can offer no relief. Given this situation, with no relief in sight, the only question that has any merit is, "How long can I tolerate this?"

Given the dilemma of a full bladder and no relief, and given the question "How long can I tolerate this?" it would be understandable to me if a person said, "I'm considering jumping off of the bridge." I would not encourage the person to jump, and I would not help him or her to jump. Furthermore, I would feel sad if the person did jump, but I would certainly understand the impulse to jump. If the person in the dilemma could become detached from reality by becoming psychotic or by chronically using drugs such as alcohol or cocaine, then the person would not have to be aware of the dilemma; but this is not the same as relief. Nor is relief to be had from well-meaning friends who encourage the person in the dilemma to "look at the bright side," because there is no bright side. There is no help in someone, out of pity, offering the person in the dilemma large sums of money so that life could be more enjoyable, for without relief there can be no joy to life. If there is to be no relief, the only thing that matters to the person in the dilemma is how long the pain can be tolerated before she or he jumps off of the bridge. This symbolically represents the human dilemma.

My view is that the natural human response to natural human events, no matter how painful, is never frightening because relief comes with time; we do not get *stuck* with pain forever. In distinct contrast, the natural human response to the unnatural event of humiliation leads to a state of alienation, helplessness, hopelessness, despair, loss of human dignity, impulses to flee or cower, rage, and impulses to seek revenge. Such responses are frightening because they seem to offer no possibility for relief. One feels *stuck* in such states indefinitely.

I will now refer to the novel *Sophie's Choice* by William Styron as a descriptive model for the human dilemma.[1] The main character, Sophie, as a What-Self, was a Roman Catholic Polish woman who lived in Cracow. Her father was a professor of law, and her husband was an instructor in mathematics at the university there. She had two small children, Jan and Eva.

German soldiers occupied Cracow in September 1939, and in November of that year the faculty of the university, including Sophie's father and husband, were ordered to assemble at the university so that they might be told of new rules for the university under the occupation. Once assembled, the faculty was suddenly forced into vans and taken to the Sachsenhausen concentration camp where, on New Year's day 1940, Sophie's father and husband were executed. For Sophie this is an experience of humiliation. She has not herself been forced to *do* anything unnatural but rather has been forced to *experience* something unnatural. It is not natural to be deprived of one's parent

---

1. William Styron, *Sophie's Choice* (New York: Random House, Inc., 1979).

or spouse by someone else's misuse of power or authority or advantage. Had Sophie's father died of pneumonia or had her husband died in an auto accident, the deaths would be tragic but *not* humiliating.

Sophie moved to Warsaw with her mother and her children. Here her mother had recurrent symptoms of tuberculosis. In response to her mother's illness, Sophie went to a small village and bought a ham. On returning to Warsaw she was stopped by Gestapo and arrested for having meat in her possession, which was against the law. In April of 1943 Sophie and her two children were sent to the Auschwitz-Birkenau concentration camp. An event at the camp gives title to the novel. After arriving by train at Auschwitz, Sophie and her children are processed along with other prisoners. Those identified as Jews or as members of the underground are sent to Birkenau to the crematoriums. When an SS[2] doctor in charge of the processing comes to Sophie, she attempts to save her children by stating that she and her children are Polish, that they are not Jewish, that they speak German, and that they are devout Catholics. After taunting Sophie for several moments the SS doctor says, "You may keep one of the children. The other one will have to go. Which one will you keep?" Sophie, in terror, shouts, "I can't choose! I can't choose!" The officer orders, "Shut up! Hurry now and choose. Choose, goddammit, or I'll send them both over." Finally,

---

2. Abbreviation for *Schutzstaffel,* Adolf Hitler's personal bodyguard in Nazi Germany.

Sophie says, "Take the baby. Take my little girl," and then watches as Eva is led away to certain death.[3]

This is Sophie's choice, and it stands as a dramatic example of humiliation. One must surely imagine that she experienced feelings of alienation, helplessness, hopelessness, despair, loss of human dignity, rage, impulses to flee or cower, and an impulse to get revenge. It may seem that there is no relief from this state, that Sophie must bear this burden forever. Sophie seems stuck in the ultimate human dilemma. Here I would point out that, although Sophie's experience is dramatic, any experience of humiliation, no matter how seemingly subtle or trivial, leads to the same dilemma.

In the novel, Sophie survives the war and eventually moves to the United States. Using the definitions of a theory on the nature of humanity, it follows that Sophie never lived again (essence) but merely survived (existence).

Before exploring for a resolution to the dilemma, one more point regarding Sophie's choice must be made. If there had been no war, no threat of war, no presence of the SS, then Sophie and her husband and children might have experienced the following: The family might have been enjoying a holiday camping in the forest, in solitude and intimacy. In this setting, if Eva were to be bitten by a poisonous insect or snake and were to die, her death would be tragic. In this

---

3. Styron, p. 589.

case, Sophie could experience her grief without fear, understanding that, in time, relief would come. Eva's death is tragic in either case, but it is not Eva's death that is the issue. It is Sophie's (and also Jan's and Eva's) humiliation that is the issue. We all eventually die. There is an end to existence, but this is natural. Humiliation is unnatural.

RESOLUTION OF THE DILEMMA

In the symbolic analogy of the full bladder, the *only* resolution to the dilemma is to urinate; that is the only relief. In the human dilemma, using Sophie's choice as an example, the *only* resolution is for Sophie to get relief from her feelings of alienation, helplessness, hopelessness, despair, rage, loss of human dignity and from her impulses to flee or to cower and to get revenge. Without such relief Sophie is stuck forever in the dilemma and can survive (existence) but cannot live (essence). Without relief, the only question of merit is how long she can tolerate the pain.

Continuing with Sophie's dilemma as a prototypic example of the ultimate human dilemma, I will now describe common examples of attempts at resolution that do not and cannot work.

REASSURANCE. It is common for us in our humanness to reach out to those in despair, to reach out to Sophie, and to offer words or actions of reassurance and comfort. We might offer her our attention and affection and encourage her to look at the bright side. We might reassure her that anyone presented with her choice might easily have acted in the same way.

We might point out to her that she was a helpless victim and therefore couldn't be responsible for what happened. These responses, no matter how caring or loving in intent, do not and cannot bring her relief. In fact, such acts might well magnify Sophie's feelings of helplessness and might make her even more uncomfortable with her feelings of rage and her vengeful impulses.

ESCAPE FROM REALITY.   If Sophie detaches herself from reality, then she may become unaware or less aware of the dilemma. If she can suppress the memory of historical events, of if she can become psychotic and thus detached from reality, or if she can use drugs in a sustained manner to blunt reality, she might become less aware of the dilemma. But these approaches are only marginally palliative. They do not and cannot bring relief.

REVENGE.   After the episode in which Sophie makes her choice, there is no further mention of the SS doctor in the novel. If Sophie were to discover that sometime later the officer had been punished for his crime either by imprisonment or by execution, or if she could herself destroy the officer, she might find some small ease of her rage and vindictiveness, but not true relief. Her despair would remain. In comparison to the analogy of the full bladder, it would be similar to urinating a few drops, which would lead only to false hope, not relief.

COMPENSATION.   If, after the war, a well-meaning person or agency, or even the SS doctor himself, were to offer Sophie a large sum of money in compensation for her loss so that she might exist in comfort, this would not and could never bring relief. Compensation does not resolve the dilemma. In fact, if Sophie were to accept such an offer, she could not spend a single penny of it without being reminded of the historical events and of her dilemma.

SUICIDE.   If Sophie jumps off of the bridge, then that is the end of her existence, but it is not a substitute for relief. Relief would lead to life (essence) without despair. It is the dilemma itself that spawns the question of how long the pain can be endured and eventually leads to the impulse to jump. If there could be relief from the dilemma, then the question of enduring pain and the impulse to jump no longer pertain. Suicide only ends existence; it does not and cannot bring relief.

FORGIVENESS.   If the SS officer were to seek out Sophie and acknowledge his act of humiliation and his state of shame, then he might ask Sophie for forgiveness. This would be, perhaps, the most that the officer could *do* as a human being. It is my view that Sophie could never offer forgiveness, the reasons for which will be addressed shortly. Of course, Sophie could answer "yes" in response to the request for forgiveness, but I do not see how such an answer could truly offer her relief from her dilemma. In fact, awareness of not being able to offer forgiveness magnifies feelings of alienation and hopelessness, magnifies the experience of being stuck in the dilemma.

Thus it would seem that neither Sophie nor the SS

doctor can *do* anything to resolve the dilemma—just as in the analogous example of the bladder there was nothing the person could *do* (to urinate) and nothing the doctor could *do* to provide relief.

I respond to Sophie in the same way I responded as a young man to seeing the films of World War II atrocities, seeing real people in real concentration camps being humiliated by real SS troops. So as not to leave the impression that I observe humiliation only from a distance, I must add that I have had my own personal experiences of humiliation, albeit not as vividly dramatic as Sophie's choice. My response is ever the same: revulsion and feelings of my own despair and helplessness and my own rage and vengefulness. I now recognize my response as an experience of my Who-Self as separate and equal and together with another Who-Self. I had no idea of what the atrocity film victims were, of their What-Selves: I did not know their names or occupations or ethnic backgrounds. But I did understand that they were human and, as Who-Selves, were separate (I felt my emotions not theirs), equal, and together (together in our humanness). If this were not true, I could watch Sophie with detached, intellectual, even scientific interest, just as I might watch an event or movie of a lion stalking, taunting, killing, and devouring a gazelle. The gazelle does not have a Who-Self that is separate and equal and together with my Who-Self. Lions killing gazelles is natural. Man humiliating Man is unnatural.

Given the earlier definition of intimacy, I now understand that my response to Sophie's dilemma is a result of my intimacy with her. Though I cannot meet Sophie face to face, I recognize that in seeing Sophie as a Who-Self I also recognize her Who-Self as separate and equal and together in relationship with my own Who-Self. I thus recognize that I am intimate with Sophie. Sophie's What-Selves and my What-Selves have no significance. I know of some of Sophie's What-Selves. Sophie is female, a daughter, a wife, a mother, Polish, Roman Catholic, a survivor of Auschwitz, and a resident of Brooklyn, but none of these facts affects my state of intimacy with Sophie as a Who-Self.

What allows the SS doctor to humiliate Sophie is that he sees her only as a worthless What-Self object and denies her Who-Self. He sees her as *untermenschen,* as less than human. He does not acknowledge her Who-Self humanness. He reacts to her existence and ignores her essence.

Since I experience myself as intimate with Sophie in acknowledging her Who-Self, I also am together with her in her dilemma. Sophie's choice and Sophie's dilemma do not have any direct effect on my existence, but they do touch me, they affect me. In my Who-Self humanness I cannot deny my state of intimacy with Sophie; I cannot choose not to be intimate with her. And therein lies the relief . . . therein lies the resolution to the human dilemma.

If I see the SS doctor as only a What-Self, as not having a Who-Self, as not being human, as being merely an *untermensch,* then I can freely humiliate or destroy him. But to do this would be to delude myself and to be as shameful as the SS doctor in his act of giving Sophie her choice. I would simply be repeating the SS doctor's sin. The history of mankind is a history of such delusions, of seeing others as What-Selves and ignoring their Who-Selves, of seeing others as black, white, red, yellow, and half-breed; as European, Asian, African; as civilized or savage; as Jew, Christian, Moslem, Hindu, atheist, or agnostic; as Fascist, Communist, Socialist, or "Free"; as male or female; as child, adolescent, or adult; as king, nobleperson, yeoman, commoner, or serf; as educated or uneducated; as good or bad; as divine or evil.

It is tempting to see the SS doctor as a savage animal, as not human, as not like me. But I can only do so by seeing him as a What-Self sans Who-Self, and I cannot so delude myself. When I see the officer as a Who-Self, as I must, then I am separate and equal and together and intimate with him exactly as I am separate and equal and together and intimate with Sophie. And just as with Sophie's dilemma, the doctor's dilemma of shame affects and includes me. So unless I deny the reality of Sophie's Who-Self and/or the reality of the doctor's Who-Self, I must in my intimacy with them share both the dilemma of despair and the dilemma of shame.

The resolution of the dilemma does not require any act, for no act or set of acts can resolve the dilemma. The resolution lies as an acceptance of what is; namely, the Who-Self. I cannot deny or change the historical fact of an act of humiliation such as Sophie's choice. I cannot approve of the doctor's act; what he did was despicable. I cannot forgive the SS doctor nor can Sophie. I cannot pretend that Sophie's dilemma does not affect and include me. What I must accept is that, in the humanness of my Who-Self, I am separate from, equal to, together with, and intimate with both Sophie and the SS doctor. In intimacy there is peace, joy, and freedom. If I see either Sophie or the SS doctor only as What-Selves and deny the reality of their Who-Selves, then there is no peace or joy or freedom, the dilemma remains unresolved, and how long I (we) can tolerate the despair and shame remains a question.

The source of humiliation and thus the source of the human dilemma is in the inequality of What-Selves. The resolution of the dilemma is in the equality of Who-Selves. The What-Self leads to alienation; the Who-Self leads to intimacy.

SUICIDE

It is my view that many if not most suicides, suicide attempts, and indeed, all forms of nonlethal, self-destructive behavior may be understood in terms of the human dilemma described above. When a person is mired in the dilemma—the despair and/or shame that results from humiliation—and when no relief is to be found, eventually the pain becomes so intolerable that jumping off the bridge seems preferable.

What is generally understood from experience in our society is that locking people up to protect them, offering reassurance and looks at the bright side, or offering a comfortable environment do not usually remove or even blunt suicidal impulses. The suicidal impulse, as an impulse, is part of the Who-Self and therefore natural, understandable, and acceptable. When a person expresses an awareness of a suicidal impulse and is told by others, directly or indirectly, that such an impulse is wrong, bad, evil, or not understandable or acceptable, then that is a denial of the person's Who-Self, which adds to humiliation.

If, when suicidal or other self-destructive impulses are expressed, one can respond with understanding and acceptance of the impulse, of the Who-Self rather than focusing on what the person does or the What-Self, then there is an opportunity to explore the suicidal person's dilemma and to offer the understanding that can lead to relief and resolution. A person's verbal expressions of an awareness of despair and impulses for suicide are most often expressions of humanness, rarely indications of illness, and never evil.

Nonlethal, self-destructive behavior may also be understood as an attempt to get relief from rage and vindictiveness without having to confront the humiliator directly either out of fear or because the humiliator is not available, as the SS doctor was not available to Sophie. This issue will be addressed further in the section on psychopathology.

Substance Abuse

The chronic, self-destructive use of drugs such as alcohol, cocaine, heroin, marijuana, tranquilizers, barbituates, and mind altering drugs such as mescaline, may be understood both as a way to detach one's self from reality, from the reality of the human dilemma, and as a way to act self-destructively in an attempt to gain some relief from the rage and vindictiveness that follows humiliation. The use of drugs may dull reality or detach the person from reality, but drugs do not resolve the dilemma. To make drugs difficult to obtain, to isolate and provide custodial care for drug users in jails or hospitals, to "train" people not to use drugs, or to broadly condemn all drug abusers as bad, evil people merely focuses on what these people do, on their What-Selves.

It is generally understood that, despite an enormous investment of effort and resources, current programs designed to treat or prevent substance abuse are not effective in any predictable, uniform manner. This is not to say that substance abuse should be approved of or encouraged. Rather, substance abuse may be understood as a human effort to escape the human dilemma. In cases where this is true—and in my view this would apply to the majority of people who abuse themselves with drugs—resolution of the dilemma should obviate the need for these drugs. The problem is what the drug users *do* in response to their pain; the resolution is to be found in who they *are*.

Psychopathology versus Human Despair

Some mental illnesses are true illnesses (psychopathology) with organic, biological causes. Examples of true psychopathology include delerium, dementia, true psychoses including schizophrenia, and the major affective disorders (manic-depressive illness). These all call for straightforward, scientific medical treatment.

It is now my view that all other psychological states may be seen as natural human responses to natural events, e.g., grief following the death of a spouse or parent or child, or as natural human responses to the unnatural event of humiliation resulting in the human dilemma. This view is consistent with the statement in the previous chapter that all psychological defense mechanisms are developed to protect against humiliation and humiliation alone.

In the United States the diagnosis of psychopathology is currently based on diagnostic criteria established by the American Psychiatric Association and published in the third edition of *Diagnostic and Statistical Manual of Mental Disorders.* These diagnostic criteria focus primarily on (1) what people do, i.e., "physical self-damaging acts" and (2) emotions, desires, and impulses that are labeled as inappropriate or abnormal, i.e., "inappropriate, intense anger." The nosology of mental illness is based on these prescriptive criteria. While such a nosology has merit as a guide for clinical study, it has the effect of directing such study along the path of scientific study, facts and knowledge, and away from the path of exploration, understanding, and wisdom. As has already been emphasized in previous chapters, one cannot understand human nature by observing and quantifying human behavior, and, further, human nature, as embodied in the Who-Self, including emotions, desires, and impulses, cannot be good or bad, cannot be normal or abnormal, cannot be sick or well.

It is possible, both in theory and in practice, to understand human despair through an understanding of human nature without recourse to a scientific construct of psychopathology. Using prescriptive criteria to identify human beings struggling with the ultimate human dilemma as being pathological only magnifies the experience of humiliation. For the person struggling with the human dilemma to be seen by a psychotherapist as a "sick" What-Self patient and for the therapist to see himself or herself as a "healthy" What-Self therapist only leads to the person remaining mired in the dilemma. Fortunately, there are many gifted therapists who are able to engage patients as equal human beings; tragically, there are many who do not. Psychotherapy has and will continue to have a significant role to play in society, but it is my view that psychotherapy must be grounded precisely in an understanding of human nature and must be conducted in the state of intimacy between two Who-Selves who are separate and equal and together. In this state, exploration from nothingness can freely occur, reconciliation can be discovered, and the dilemma can be resolved.

IDENTITY CONFUSION

The genesis of identity confusion will be described under "Child Development." For now let it be stated that the distinction between the Who-Self and the What-Self is precisely the point of our individual identities; identity confusion derives from any distortion of that distinction. If one is aware of and understands who one is and, in contrast, knows what one is, there is no identity confusion. Three major types of identity confusion will now be considered.

One type of identity confusion occurs when the Who-Self is treated as a What-Self resulting in attempts to see the Who-Self as a matter of choice or will, as explainable and as measurable. This leads to the Who-Self being experienced erroneously as an object and therefore subject to rejection. In this state of confusion there can be no intimacy, no freedom, no peace, and no happiness.

Another form of identity confusion is based in the learned belief that what you do matters and who you are does not matter. To state this another way, all that matters is being a successful What-Self. This erroneous, destructive view gives rise to people focusing all of their energies on being good enough What-Selves. Many people are able to achieve success in surviving (existence) in style and comfort, but never in living (essence). Such people may invest considerable money and effort on "leisure" activities in which they continue to work at being good enough, but in which they never or rarely experience solitude or intimacy.

The third type of identity confusion is found in the nonspecific or generic What-Self. Such a person is generally timid, passive, and fearful. Somehow these persons have learned to ignore any specificity of what they are, including the need for explicit, fair, and uniformly applied measurements specific to a specific What-Self. They see everyone, including perfect strangers, as having equal authority, power, or advantage to reject or to humiliate them. This distorts and magnifies the risk of rejection and humiliation and leads to constant vigilance and apprehension. For example, in a classroom a generic What-Self student experiences the other students as having as much authority and power as the professor.

IDENTICAL TWINS

Brief mention needs be made of identical twins in this regard. It is common knowledge that identical twins experience life in ways subtly different from the ways in which other people experience it. At various times in history some cultures have attributed mystical, magical powers to identical twins. In the field of psychology there is a specific body of literature about identical twins including views about how psychotherapy with an identical twin doesn't quite work in the same manner as psychotherapy with others. In my own experience as a therapist, I have found working with identical twins to be a fascinating and an extraordinarily difficult experience.

The unique human quality of identical twins might be understood within the context of the theory of human nature herein presented. In the previously described developmental process of separation, identical twins may progressively see themselves as separate from their mother, but separate as a matched, identical set, a set that has a oneness about it. Concurrently, in the developmental process of individuation identical twins may progressively experience themselves as uniquely different from their mother and others, but not uniquely different from one another. Thus, at the termination of separation–individuation, identical twins may see themselves as What-Selves separate from their mother and as Who-Selves uniquely different from their mother, but with their own Who-Self fused and with an additional nonchoice What-Self of being a matched set. In my view, understanding this fusion and matching of identical twins could lead to a clearer understanding of the dynamics of identical twins.

CHILD DEVELOPMENT

It seems without controversy that the misadventures of childhood are the spawning grounds of many adult miseries. The newborn infant is helpless and dependent. The adult must be autonomous and resourceful. The path from childhood to adulthood is fraught with peril and, in view of our human fallibility, mistakes are inevitable. However, errors arising from human fallibility are distinctly different from errors of omission or commission.

There is a legal principle that if, as a victim of a crime, you put yourself "in harm's way," the accused wrong doer can be absolved. Since the child is "in harm's way" in its trek to adulthood, and since parents are solely responsible for having placed the child "in harm's way," then it is the parents' beholden duty to protect the child from harm and in no case to be the source of harm.

The discussion of child development presented in the context of a theory on the nature of humanity will offer a way to understand some of the risks of development. It should follow that any understanding of such risks from this view must, perforce, include clarity of distinction between errors of parental human fallibility and errors of parental omission or commission.

Earlier it was noted that the intrapsychic process of separation–individuation occurring between the fourth month and third year of life has been called the psychological birth of the child. There is need for continued efforts to refine and clarify our understanding of this early stage of child development. It is my view that the current understanding of child development up to the phase of separation-individuation is basically sound, but as I have already noted, my view of the effect of separation-individuation varies markedly from present psychodynamic theories. The discussion of child development presented here focuses on events that occur following separation-individuation or following the child's awareness of its Who-Self and its What-Self.

The newborn infant is helpless and incapable of autonomous survival. The infant is totally dependent. The three-year-old What-Self has some limited capacity for being a good enough What-Self for survival; for example, a three-year-old has some language skills and can ask for what he or she needs or wants. However, the child remains highly dependent and cannot survive on its own. By societal norms, as embodied in common law (law based on custom), children attain adulthood at about age eighteen. Historically there have been times when many children were expected to survive on their own at a much earlier age, as young as eight or ten, and even today there are areas where "street children" exist. But this violates the current societal norm.

The What-Self child has nearly eighteen years to become good enough to survive autonomously, eighteen years to develop intellect, physical strength, coordination, fine motor skills, and language skills and to develop an understanding of the What-Self existence of being measured and of being good enough (accountability). At the end of this period of development the What-Self adult must survive on her or his own.

The development of the What-Self child may be defined most simply as a process of accruing survival skills in anticipation of attaining autonomous What-

Self adulthood. Many, and perhaps the majority, of these necessary survival skills accrue from exploration, which leads to understanding, wisdom, and maturity. Many fewer of these skills come from didactic learning, which, of course, only leads to knowledge. The public school system is surely privy to an extraordinarily different understanding of child development.

The What-Self child is one of the two exceptions to the definition of the What-Self as a choice, whereas the What-Self parent is definitely a matter of choice. It has been shown that the What-Self is for survival, and yet the What-Self child cannot survive alone; its survival is dependent on the What-Self parents. This dependency, absolute in the beginning, diminishes over time as the child develops survival skills of its own. The What-Self parent is not completely autonomous for the parent must be good enough to ensure survival and existence for both self and child. With regard to survival the child is "in harm's way" and must be protected by its parents. As the child practices each new skill, the parent's protection *must* diminish over time so that the What-Self child may attain adulthood full blown and beyond practicing. One of the potential errors of parenthood, clearly not attributable to human fallibility, is to maintain the same level of protection, the same level of responsibility for survival, throughout childhood, and thus interfere with the child's What-Self testing and practicing hard-earned skills.

The What-Self parent does, however, have the re-sponsibility and authority to measure the What-Self child and to decide what is good enough. As in all What-Self experiences, the measurements must be explicit, fair, and uniformly applied. It is from the What-Self parent that the What-Self child first experiences the requirement to be good enough to survive. Since, initially, the child is totally dependent on its parents for survival, the lesson of being good enough is easily learned. It must be stressed that as the child's skills increase and as the parents' responsibilities for survival diminish, so too must the parents' authority and power diminish. Another potential error of parenting is to maintain a uniform stance of power and authority throughout the period of childhood (and sometimes beyond), thus progressively infantalizing the developing child and demeaning the child's increasing skills.

It is appropriate and necessary for parents to exercise their authority and to be clear about whether the child's What-Self skills are good enough. Survival is dependent on being good enough as an adult What-Self; the more clearly the child comes to understand and accept that reality, the more prepared she or he will be to accept the stripes of adulthood. If the child does not come to understand this, the state of being "in harm's way" is extended beyond the protection of childhood.

The What-Self child, like any What-Self, is at risk of rejection, and such rejection is necessary and valu-

able. The experience of being measured, which leads
to criticism, rejection or acceptance, and discrimination, is necessary in order to survive in the adult world.
Parents have a responsibility to provide these measurements during childhood to prepare the child for adulthood. This parental responsibility is shared, in lesser
degree, by other adults in the child's life, particularly
by teachers.

The What-Self child is also at risk of humiliation
and, because of its dependency on others for survival
(being a developing, unfinished What-Self), the time
of childhood holds a greater risk of humiliation than
any other period of life by some magnitude. It will
be noted, without comment, that it is a grievous parental error of omission to fail to protect the child
from humiliation from others and an even more grievous error of commission to be the cause of any
humiliating experience for the child.

In its simplest form, the relationship between parent
and child may be stated in terms of the What-Self
parents' responsibility to *take care of* the nonchoice
What-Self child while the child What-Self develops
survival skills and an understanding of the need to be
good enough.

There are, of course, potential hazards to the child
during the process of separation-individuation, including some of those mentioned above. For present
purposes I will assume the absence of mishaps during
separation-individuation. Given this premise, the
child's Who-Self arrives by age three in full blossom;

there is nothing more to understand; there are no skills to be acquired. The child Who-Self is fully aware of his or her unique perceptions, tastes, values, emotions, desires, fantasies, and impulses. These will change over time with growth throughout life, but they will never be more complete. The child Who-Self, as with any other Who-Self, is dissimilar from and equal to all other Who-Selves including its parents' Who-Selves. Free of responsibility for survival, in view of its undeveloped What-Self survival skills and the availability of parental What-Self skills, the child is marvelously free to explore the immediate environment—all of the sights, sounds, smells, tastes, and textures available. During this time, exploration, no matter how active, is peaceful, free, happy, and mindless.

Since, by present definition, all that one can do with the Who-Self is to understand and accept it, then the only thing available in the Who-Self child-parent relationship is to experience intimacy. In this relationship, living—the essence of life—can be enriched and enhanced for both child and parent. This is the joy of childhood and of parenthood. Intimacy, of course, requires parent and child to be oblivious to their What-selves. For the child, such obliviousness comes naturally. There is little else that can be said about the relationship; all one can do is experience and savor it.

In its simplest form the Who-Self function of the parent may be defined as *caring about* the child. In contrast to the *taking-care-of* function of the What-Self parent, which diminishes over time and stops when the child attains adulthood, the *caring-about* function of the Who-Self parent is constant over time and need never stop. Sustained intimate relationships are precious; to have a life-long intimate relationship with one's parents and one's children is to be at least twice blessed.

For the parent-child relationship to function as described, the distinction between the Who-Self and What-Self of both parent and child must be kept clear. One of the major errors of parenting, an error not ascribable to human fallibility, is for parents to blur the Who-Self What-Self distinction and thereby *teach* their child to blur or lose the distinction between its own Who-Self and What-Self. Children, and most adults for that matter, can and will *learn* anything, including utter nonsense. Learning only leads to knowledge, and you don't have to understand knowledge.

Following are some examples of how the distinction between the Who-Self and What-Self may become blurred or lost during childhood.

> EXAMPLE: If mother says to child, "We are leaving early tomorrow morning to spend the weekend with Aunt Martha," the child may respond with, "I hate Aunt Martha, I don't like going there. I want to stay home and play with my friends. If you make me go you're a mean mommy." This is a pure expression of the child's Who-Self and, as noted previously, the Who-Self can only be understood and accepted. Mother's or any other adult's response to the child is crucial.

Mother may respond with, "I'm glad you told me that. It's important for me to understand how you feel and how you see things, because how I feel and how I see things may be different, and the only way that I can understand that is if you tell me. You do have to go to Aunt Martha's with us because children [as What-Selves] must do things that their parents tell them to do, but it is important to me to understand that you don't want to go and that you're angry because I am telling you that you must go." This response addresses both the Who-Self and the What-Self of the child in its understanding and acceptance of the expression of the child's Who-Self. It is also a proper expression of parental What-Self authority. Moreover, the mother is revealing her own distinction between Who-Self and What-Self. She is indicating to the child that she has her own feelings, views, and desires that are dissimilar from and equal to her child's and that her What-Self parent has the authority to demand compliance.

A second mother might respond with, "Oh my! Then we won't go." This response conveys to the child that the child's Who-Self is powerful which, in reality, it cannot be. The response also conveys to the child that it isn't necessary to be measured and criticized as a What-Self. Furthermore, the response does not provide the child with any clear picture of the mother's Who-Self What-Self dichotomy.

A third mother might respond with, "Shame on you! How dare you say that! Your Aunt Martha loves you; she sends you beautiful presents for your birthday and at Christmas. I can't imagine a child of mine having such evil thoughts. I don't ever want to hear anything like that again." This response conveys to the child that her or his Who-Self can be bad and unacceptable, neither one of which is true by definition. Her message is that the child had better be a good What-Self child, and that she's not interested in hearing about the child's Who-Self. If children receive consistent messages of this type, they learn to treat their Who-Selves as if they were What-Selves—as if their Who-Selves could be a choice, could be explained, and could be bad. In such cases, all of the child's creative effort of separation-individuation is lost, resulting in a life of confusion and despair; the child survives only as a What-Self. The psychological birth of the child has been aborted.

EXAMPLE: A father tells his son, age thirteen, "Tomorrow is trash day and I'm giving you the responsibility to take the trash out to the curb." This is an appropriate use of parental authority. If the son doesn't get the trash out on time or only gets part of it out, then the father has the responsibility and the authority to say, "That's not good enough. From now on you will have to have all of the trash out on time, and if you fail in that I will withhold one half of your allowance." That same afternoon the father and son can go fishing and have a time of intimacy and can keep the two experiences distinguishable. Taking out the trash is part of What-Self existence and going fishing is part of Who-Self essence. In such a case, the distinction between Who-Self and What-Self remains clear for both father and son.

Suppose, however, that on discovering the son's failure the father says, "You worthless oaf! Can't you ever do anything around here? Are you stupid or something? I guess I'll have to take out the trash since I can't count on you." This is not only an abrogation of the father's proper authority and power, it is a misuse of that authority in an act of humiliation.

Or perhaps the father says, "Well since you didn't find the time or energy to get the trash out, then we'll just cancel the fishing trip." This again is an abrogation of proper authority and sows the seeds of the son's learning that he has to be a good enough What-Self to get love (intimacy) rather than to survive. To put it another way, the Who-Self is invalidated because the What-Self has failed.

Or the father might say, "After all I've done for you, I'd think you could do a simple thing like take the trash out for me." This ignores the What-Self responsibility of both father and son.

The father is required to *take care of* the son as a What-Self father, and the son is supposed to take the trash out because that is what is required to be a good enough What-Self son learning the ropes of the What-Self world on his way to adulthood. Being a good enough What-Self does *not* obligate anyone else to be good enough in return. The father implies that since he is good enough as a father, the son owes it him to be good enough in return. This ignores the father's authority.

EXAMPLE: A seven-year-old girl, home from school, is sitting at the window in solitude watching the rain. Mother says one or more of the following: "Are you bored dear?" "Is there something the matter, are you ill?" "Can't you find something to do besides just sitting?" "Since you aren't doing anything why don't you go straighten up your room." "How can you just sit there? When I was your age I had a hundred chores to do when I got home from school." All of these ignore the value of solitude and thus the value of the Who-Self. They also place emphasis on things that should be done as a What-Self, but without using the available parental authority to tell the girl what is expected.

EXAMPLE: Parent says to child or children or spouse or neighbor or writes in a magazine article, "I feel so unappreciated. I work so hard to do things for you and to make things nice for you and you don't seem to care." This conveys the message that since the speaker is such a good What-Self (I *take care of you*), the person being addressed should show that he or she *cares*. This treats the Who-Self function of *caring about* and the What-Self function of *taking care of* as if they were one and the same, thus blurring the distinction between the Who-Self and the What-Self.

EXAMPLE: A six-year-old child gets a birthday "gift" and hears from her parents, "Now that cost lots of money [What-Self survival stuff], so take care of it...you have to be careful and not break it...don't take it outdoors, it might get lost...don't let your friends play with it, they might break it...you can't play with it until you put your other toys away." The child hears this as a challenge to be good enough, a chance to practice survival skills. The child would be hard pressed to experience the gift as a Who-Self act of *caring* and at best would be confused about the Who-Self What-Self dichotomy. Such statements also make clear to the child that the "gift" doesn't belong to himself or herself, that it still belongs to the "giver."

EXAMPLE: Mother says to son or father says to daughter, "Your mother (father) works so hard to make things nice for us. Can't you show your appreciation by doing something nice once in awhile?" Once again love and caring (Who-Self) are connected with and thus confused with being good enough (What-Self).

EXAMPLE: In general, when a child hears its experience of solitude characterized as "lazy" or "unappreciative" and its experiences of exploration described as "mischievous" or "troublesome," and when the child is told that the he or she is responsible for the burden of parenthood, which was the parents' choice, then it is easy to understand how the distinction between Who-Self and What-Self, between essence and existence, gets blurred or lost.

There is a lexicon of judgmental descriptors that, when used by parents, can so confuse a child's sense of Who-Self and What-Self that the child may spend the rest of life in some degree of confusion. The following words are powerful and destructive when they are used to describe the child's experiences of solitude or intimacy or lack of success in a What-Self task and even more destructive when the Who-Self What-Self dichotomy of either the parent or the child is not clear: bad, naughty, nasty, wicked, evil, monstrous, hideous, outrageous, atrocious, not nice, horrid, ugly, terrible, shocking, mean, unmanageable, shameful, difficult, dreadful, sinful, wretched, and selfish. None of these words applies in any way to the Who-Self, since the Who-Self cannot be measured and cannot be good or bad. If the What-Self child has not been good enough, has failed, and if the measurements have been explicit and fair and the parent has properly used his or her authority, then the clear statement "that's not good enough" should be totally sufficient.

A particular mention must be made about selfishness. It is common to hear people express the view that selfishness is bad. Included in this view is the supposition that the opposite of selfish is to be giving and kind. What I have come to understand is that people who describe selfishness as bad are often those who have lost distinction between their own Who-Self and What-Self. To them, the way to avoid selfishness is to be a good, indeed *very* good, What-Self and to deny the Who-Self. So, in fact, the opposite of selfishness is to be *selfless,* to be without a Who-Self. The dictionary definition of *selfish* fits the lexicon of human denouncements in saying that to be selfish is to be "devoted to or concerned with one's own advantage or welfare to the exclusion of regard for others." But the dictionary also defines *selfless* as "having no regard for a thought of self; unselfish."[4] If, in fact, the stem word *self* refers to the Who-Self, then it would follow that being aware of the Who-Self is selfish and bad, while not being aware of the Who-Self is selfless and good. I clearly take exception to this view. If, however, the stem word *self* refers to the What-Self, then the definitions are easily in agreement with my views.

I will now return to the statement of Erik Erikson cited previously. Here I will underscore certain words and will add parenthetical comments. On the basis of what has been presented in this theory, I believe Erik-

---

4. *The Shorter Oxford English Dictionary* (London: Clarendon Press, 1984), p. 1934.

son's original statement may now be understood in quite a different light.

"But the fact remains that the human being in early childhood *learns* to consider one or the other aspect of bodily function as *evil, shameful,* or *unsafe.* There is no culture which does not *use* a combination of these *devils* to develop, by way of counterpoint, its own style of faith, pride, certainty, and initiative. Thus there remains in man's sense of *achievement* the suspicion of its infantile roots; and since his earliest sense of reality was *learned* by the painful testing of inner and outer *goodness* and *badness* [there can be no inner Who-Self goodness or badness], man remains ready to expect from some enemy [a What-Self], force, or event [rejection] in the outer world that which, in fact, endangers him from within: from his own angry drives [which come in response to humiliation which comes from without], from his own sense of smallness [only the What-Self can be relatively small; the Who-Self is equal] and from his own *split* inner world [the split is natural]. Thus he is always irrationally [not in my view] ready to fear invasion [humiliation] by vast and vague forces which are other than himself; strangling encirclement by everything that is not safely classified as allied; and devastating loss of face before all-surrounding, mocking audiences [humiliation]. These [fears of humiliation], not the animal's fears, characterize human anxiety, and this in world affairs as well as in personal affairs."[5]

---

5. Erik Erikson, *Childhood and Society* (2d ed.; New York: W.W. Norton & Co., Inc., 1963), p. 406. Italics and bracketed comments are mine.

The examples are endless and the results are easily predictable and understandable. Any confusion between the nature and function of the Who-Self and the nature and function of the What-Self leads to confusion and the inability to experience freedom, peace, and happiness. The What-Self is vulnerable to and can also inflict humiliation; the What-Self destroys solitude and intimacy. The Who-Self destroys nothing.

THE FAMILY

Of all societal units, the family—whether conventional, single-parent, or extended—is the best suited to ensuring the essence of living, solitude and intimacy, and caring about and loving. The family, in intimacy, is peaceful and free and happy. The family must understand that *being* who you are matters, and *doing* what you do doesn't matter. This is not to say that family members should be indifferent to what other members do; only that they must understand that essence is more important than existence.

The What-Self parent in the role of taking care of the What-Self child until the child becomes an autonomous adult has important responsibilities. All of these responsibilities, as well as What-Self responsibilities outside the family, can be fulfilled within the context that who one is matters and what one does does not matter.

EXAMPLE: The dishes. Dishes don't matter; they do not have to be washed. Dishes don't care whether or not they are clean or dirty. They never say "Please wash me, I'm dirty." Dishes are washed because of a Who-Self value of liking to eat off of clean dishes. It is the Who-Self value that matters, not what you do or don't do with the dishes.

A spouse who likes to have clean dishes has several choices. He or she may choose to wash the dishes or may ask his or her spouse, or someone else for that matter, to wash them. In asking one's spouse to wash the dishes, one is entitled to a yes or no answer, just as in any intimate relationship one may ask for anything one wants and is entitled to a yes or no answer. Either answer, yes or no, is totally sufficient. If the spouse says yes, then the dishes will be washed because someone has chosen to wash them, not because the dishes *need* to be washed. If the spouse says no, then the one who has asked may choose to wash the dishes or leave them unwashed. The dishes still don't *need* to be washed. Since spouses are equal as Who-Selves, neither has the authority to tell the other that they have to do the dishes; a Who-Self spouse in intimacy may only ask.

With dependent children the parent has two choices. One choice is to ask, "Will you wash the dishes?" Here again one is entitled to a yes or no answer. And again, either answer, yes or no, is acceptable. In making the other choice, the parent says to a child, "You are to wash the dishes tonight." Here the parent is using his or her authority appropriately to instruct the child what to do. Further, the parent has the authority to explicitly state the precise measurements of how the dishes are to be washed, dried, and put away—measurements of what is good enough. If, in response to being told to do the dishes, the child says, "I hate doing dishes," or "I did them last night, so I don't think it is fair that I have to do them tonight," the child is expressing the Who-Self, which matters and must be understood and accepted. Doing the dishes doesn't matter. The dishes don't *need* to be done. The child must, of course, do the dishes, and do them according to the explicit standards stated by the parent, because the child has been told to do so by the parent. But the dishes are done within the context of the understanding that who the child is matters and doing the dishes doesn't matter.

Statements such as the following are often made about the dishes, but none of them is consistent with a state of intimacy. "I'd like for you to do the dishes" or "I wish someone would do the dishes tonight" are both expressions of the Who-Self and require only the response of being understood. They are not requests inviting a yes or no response, and they are not commands requiring action. "The dishes need to be done so someone is going to have to do them" is a nonsensical statement requiring no response, because the dishes do not *need* to be done; the dishes don't matter. "After all the work I do around here, you'd think someone might offer to do the dishes once in awhile" is a meaningless statement because working doesn't commit someone else to think in response, while asking someone else to do the dishes does commit them to a yes or no response; or if you have authority (a parent to a child or a What-Self employer to a What-Self dishwasher) you can tell them to do the dishes. "When's the last time you did a dish around here?" simply requires a factual response of date and time without further explanation.

EXAMPLE: Gifts. In the intimacy of family one gives a gift because it feels loving to do that. As an expression of the Who-Self the gift matters, but the giving of it doesn't matter. The recipient of the gift accepts and understands the gift as an expression of the giver's Who-Self, and it doesn't matter what the recipient *does* with the gift. Who you are matters and what you do doesn't matter.

Often a thing is offered under the guise of being a gift but with the implied message to the recipient that "if you really love me you will treasure this and take care of it." Such an offering is not a gift; it is a burden—something to be taken care of properly to demonstrate caring. The message is that what the recipient does with the object falsely called a gift is more important than who the recipient is. Taking care of is a What-Self function, and *caring about* is a Who-Self function.

In summary, the family, in understanding that individual Who-Selves matter equally and that what they do doesn't matter, can live in intimacy, with freedom and without fear, with peacefulness and without rancor, with joy and without despair.

LOVE

Love is intimacy; intimacy is love. Love is the essence of being and not in existence and doing. Love is the enhancement of solitude by the presence, in being, of another or others. The Who-Self in solitude is constantly, irrevocably, absolutely lovely and loveable. Two (or more) Who-Selves in concert in intimacy accept each other as equally absolutely lovely and loveable. One cannot earn love by being a good enough What-Self. One can only *accept* love in the intimacy of equal Who-Selves. To label a husband, a wife, or a marriage "good" or a child "good" or "bad" is antithetical to intimacy and love. The Who-Self can be neither good nor bad, but is constantly, irrevocably, absolutely lovely and loveable. The love in intimacy is unfailingly available. Love can be ignored by looking at the What-Self, but the love cannot be destroyed; love and intimacy always are.

EQUALITY

Who-Selves are equal; What-Selves are unequal. The equality of Who-Selves allows the peacefulness and beauty of intimacy and love. The inequality of What-Selves allows power, rejection, humiliation, despair, and shame.

Throughout the course of history, specific What-Self groups have banded together in response to experiences of humiliation and have demanded equality. Such groups give rise to causes, movements, and even wars. Each group demands that the rights of its members be equal to the rights of the members of some other group, with membership in both groups determined by a specific What-Self. Such causes rarely fail to touch our humanness; they stir our deepest emotions. How can one argue with the simple beauty and elegance of *Liberte!, Egalité! Fraternité!?* Despite the obvious humanness of such movements and their mobilization of intelligence, dedication, sacrifice, and even heroic valor, these struggles seem to go on endlessly, and the results seem marginal at best.

Three such movements will be considered here as examples of how social movements do not and cannot work as solutions to the human dilemma given their present premises and seen in the light of a theory on the nature of humanity. Although each movement purports to offer a solution to the human dilemma, each offers only What-Self solutions to What-Self problems.

The Women's Movement

Without fear of contradiction, I will offer the view that women have long been subjects of humiliation. Historically, they have been seen as somehow "less" than men. Moreover, they have been seen primarily by men, and often by themselves, as What-Selves, measured in terms of whether they are "good" wives, "good" mothers, "good" neighbors, "good" hostesses, "good" sex partners, and so onward ad nauseum. In being seen as "less" than men, whatever that means, and as being seen as What-Selves, women are, of course, chronically at the risk of rejection and humiliation. Women's rage and vengefulness in response to humiliation are all too easily understandable, are expressions of their humanness, and are to be celebrated.

The Women's Movement seeks revenge for the humiliation of women by looking for equality in the work place, in professions, in government, in religion, in social settings ("don't open the door for me, I can do it myself"), and in the home. In so far as it fights for the equal administration of rules and measurements in the What-Self world—and sex is not a basis of measurement—the Women's Movement is to be applauded. By definition, however, equality— whether of rights, pay, status, or independence—cannot exist in a world that functions on the basis of What-Selves, for example in the workplace world. We can attempt to apply standards of measurement equally and fairly to What-Selves, e.g., to reward work done to the same specifications with the same rate of pay, but this will not obviate hierarchies of What-Selves. In the inequality of the What-Self world, great care must be used in applying measurements to determine such things as rights, pay, status, and independence because everyone subject to such judgments is at great risk of humiliation. Causes such as the

Women's Movement insist on the uniform application of such measurements, but their fight treats only the What–Self world. The resolution of the human dilemma is not to be found in that world.

The resolution of the human dilemma lies in understanding and accepting that which is: that, as Who–Selves, we are constantly, irrevocably, absolutely lovely and loveable, regardless of What–Self descriptors such as sex. We are equal in who we are, which matters, and unequal in what we do, which does not matter. A woman who is a lousy cook or who is unfairly discriminated against in her law firm remains constantly lovely and equal as a Who–Self. When a woman looks in a mirror, all that she sees is the visage of a female *Homo sapiens* What–Self; nobody can see a Who–Self in a mirror. If women would focus on who they are instead of what they are, the resolution of their dilemma would be at hand.

If I embrace the Women's Movement as a What–Self male *Homo sapiens,* I remain alienated from women, whereas if I embrace it as a Who–Self, I am one with women. It only matters who you are; it doesn't matter what you do—including whether or not you open doors or have them opened for you.

The Civil Rights Movement

Again without fear of contradiction, I will offer the view that Blacks in this country and elsewhere have long been the subjects of humiliation. This humiliation stems primarily from the nonchoice What–Self of being a variety of *Homo sapiens* with darkly pigmented skin. Historically, Blacks in the United States have been seen as "less" than whites, which makes as much sense, or rather nonsense, as seeing women as somehow "less" than men. It also leads to awkward combinations and permutations of evaluation on the basis of What-Self differences of skin color in combination with differences of sex, for example, white women being seen as both "more" and "less" than black men and white men being seen as "more" than black women on two counts. A much higher order of mathematics is needed to sort out where mulattoes, yet another variation of a nonchoice What-Self, fit in such a more-than less-than absurdity.

The point remains that in any What-Self description, such as blackness, there is inequality by definition, and this provides a basis for discrimination. It is a matter of simple observation for me to discriminate a black person as darker in skin color than myself. This discriminating observation does not, however, give me the authority or power to discriminate *against* someone who is darker than myself. I cannot ignore my perception of different skin color, but my perception, a function of my Who-Self, does not give me any authority or power, What-Self functions, to order ebony Blacks to sit at the back of a bus, mulattoes to sit in the middle of a bus, and albinos to sit at the very front of a bus. Blacks, in who they are, are constantly, irrevocably, absolutely, and equally lovely and loveable, as are all other Who-Selves.

Blacks, like women and others who have been unfairly discriminated against, have rallied together in their response to humiliation and their collective despair. They have demanded equality with rage and vengefulness. Their rage and vengefulness are understandably human, and their feelings of rage and impulses to get revenge are to be celebrated. The nondestructive verbal expressions of these feelings and impulses are clear, unequivocal demonstrations of their humanness, demonstrations of their togetherness with all other humans who experience humiliation; they are not demonstrations of subhuman savagery.

In the United States, chronic humiliation of Blacks spawned the Civil Rights Movement. Like women, Blacks have focused on the equality of What-Selves. Where one sits on a bus, where one eats, where one lives, and where one goes to school—although necessarily free choices in a free society—do not in and of themselves lead to equality. In fact, some literal applications of equality of opportunity to What-Selves may magnify humiliation. For example, under the rubric of affirmative-action programs, a university admissions office may purposely overlook a student's educational inadequacies and grant the student admission on the basis of the student's What-Self blackness. That student may thus be unable to meet the demands (measurements) of the university and be at the risk of further humiliation. Some militants (powerful What-Selves) of the Civil Rights Movement have implied that because of a history of deprivation (humiliation), Blacks in certain work and educational settings should not be measured in any way, no matter how explicit, fair, or uniformly applied the measurements might be. Human society can and must work toward the fair and impartial measuring of What-Selves. The determination of a "good enough" physician or student or citizen must be based on criteria specific to physicians, or students, or citizens. The potential for humiliation is only magnified if a different set of measurements is applied to black physicians, to women physicians, to foreign medical graduate physicians, or to white Anglo-Saxon male physicians. Measurements to determine whether or not a physician What-Self is "good enough" should measure that and only that.

The resolution of the human dilemma is the same for Blacks as it is for women or anyone: to accept that which already is, the absolute equality of Who-Selves. The visage of a black face in the mirror is merely a reflection of a What-Self; no one can see a Who-Self in a mirror. The Who-Self is always understandable, always acceptable, and always beautiful. That black is beautiful is a matter of taste; that a Who-Self is beautiful is a matter of truth. As a "whitey" What-Self, I remain alienated from Blacks. As a Who-Self, despite my white Anglo-Saxonness, I can embrace and be embraced by Who-Selves who happen to be described as black. It only matters who you are; it doesn't matter what you do—including where you sit on a bus.

The Labor Movement

Again without fear of contradiction, I will offer the view that laborers have long been subjects of humiliation. Karl Marx described with great clarity what happened historically in the transition from an hierarchical feudal system in which serfs were at the bottom of the hierarchy to the hierarchical capitalist industrial system in which the serfs became free citizens but free only to sell themselves to the highest bidding capitalist. That capitalist management What-Selves misused their positions of power and advantage to humiliate the working class is a matter of history. The common laborer, lacking training in intellectual skills or specialized manual skills, became an expendable pawn. Again the focus was on what one could do or not do without heed to who one was. In this setting, what one did mattered and who one was didn't matter. Karl Marx's proposed resolution was to make everybody equal as What-Selves, and the Labor Movement, which is based on Marx's ideas, doesn't work for that very reason. Socialism and Communism did not and will not lead to the Garden of Eden. They lead instead to the Tower of Babel.

At this point I will insert an historical note in an attempt to underscore the togetherness of Who-Selves. During the colonial period in the United States, some of my ancestors were slave owners. In being separate and equal and together with these ancestors, I must share in their shame. At precisely the same time in history, other of my ancestors were colliers (coal miners) in Scotland, existing under law as hereditary serfs. In being separate and equal and together with these ancestors, I must share in their despair. My Scottish ancestors were, by law, emancipated from serfdom in 1799, just sixty-three years before President Abraham Lincoln emancipated the slaves in this country.

A casual look at Socialism, Communism, and even the Democratic Labor Movement in this country shows results that are characterized by alienation, despair, anger, and destructive behavior rather than by freedom or peacefulness. In attempting to make What-Selves equal, which in reality is not possible, such movements undermine accountability and responsibility among employees by attacking the use of measurements, criticism, rejection (firing), and fair discrimination as tools by which to evaluate whether they are "good enough." No matter how explicit, fair, and uniformly applied measurements may be in the workplace, it is nearly impossible to fire an employee, whether laborer or manager, without facing litigation in the name of "human rights." It has become a national tragedy that such ideals are used to keep unqualified people in jobs.

The resolution for the workers is the same as for women and Blacks and others: to focus on the equality and the innate beauty of the Who-Self. In so doing, the laborer may face the boss as an equal Who-Self and continue to work in the hierarchy of society focusing secondarily on the fairness of measurements. Marx was surely aware of the intrinsic value and beauty of individual human beings, as he was aware of the despair of common laborers in their humiliation. But the resolution does not and cannot come from any attempt to make What-Selves equal. The resolution comes from accepting that which already is, the equality of the Who-Self. It only matters who you are, it doesn't matter what you do—whether you work on an assembly line or in executive office suite.

EDUCATION AND KNOWLEDGE

Education is for the teaching and learning of knowledge and/or acquired technical skills. Knowledge allows one to know about things, but does not lead to understanding or wisdom. In our educational system we treat children as computers by asking them to memorize, store, and retrieve knowledge. All too often teachers are dismayed to find that these computers are indeed alive with lively minds and with impulses to explore. It is here, in the formal educational system, that children are often told that what you do (learning, storing, and retrieving knowledge) matters, and who you are (being, living, exploring) doesn't matter. All too many children learn this awful message, ignore who they are (which really does matter), and march onward to success as good student What-Selves by doing the right things (which doesn't matter).

My favorite book on education is *The Aims of Education* by Alfred North Whitehead. Whitehead was a mathematician turned philosopher What-Self, but in his writings his marvelous Who-Self always shone brightly through. One brief quotation is offered here:

There is only one subject matter for education, and that is life in all of its manifestations. Instead of this simple unity, we offer children Algebra, from which nothing follows; Geometry, from which nothing follows; Science, from which nothing follows; History, from which nothing follows; a couple of Languages, never mastered; and lastly, most dreary of all, Literature, represented by plays of Shakespeare, with philological notes and short analyses of plot and character to be in substance committed to memory."[6]

I do not wish in any way to diminish the value of education and knowledge, but rather to put them into a proper perspective that would include exploration for understanding and wisdom as far more valuable than learning and knowledge. In the past century what we have learned about the universe, what we know, has increased at a truly staggering rate, but there is little to suggest that we are any more wise for it.

Education would be exceedingly more valuable, and indeed exceedingly more palatable, if it were merely presented for what it is; presented as a way to know about the universe in the service of the What-Self function of survival and existence. If this were made clear, then exploration for understanding and wisdom could continue in parallel without confusion. There is nothing particularly wrong with having knowledge, with knowing about, just as there is nothing wrong with surviving in comfort and physical

6. Alfred North Whitehead, *The Aims of Education* (New York: Macmillan Co., 1929), p. 10.

well being. But there is no wisdom, no happiness, no peace, no freedom in merely knowing about and in surviving in comfort. It is possible, and in my view desirable and necessary, for the What-Self to be educated, to learn, to know about, but not at the expense of the Who-Self's exploration for understanding.

THE NATURAL SCIENCES

The natural sciences—biology, chemistry, mathematics, and physics—enable us to know about the universe including our What-Self bodies. But all that can come from the study of the natural sciences is knowledge. Through the study of the natural sciences I can know about the forest without leaving my study, but to understand the forest I must leave my study to explore it. As a medical student, through the study of anatomy, embryology, histology, neuroanatomy, physiology, biochemistry, pathology, microbiology, medicine, surgery, pediatrics, neurology, and obstetrics, I came to *know* about Man, but this did not lead to an understanding of human nature. It was only when I left my study and my studies and explored from nothingness in my consulting room that I came to some understanding of the nature of humanity.

Here I would add that mathematics fits uneasily into the natural sciences. It is true that measurement enables the other natural sciences to quantify and to know about the universe, and there is knowledge within mathematics itself. But mathematics also leads to exploration beyond knowing. It is, perhaps, the concept of 0 or nothingness in mathematics that not only allows but calls for exploration. It is not by chance that mathematicians, such as Whitehead, often came eventually to philosophy and the business of wisdom.

THE SOCIAL SCIENCES

My experience as an undergraduate was that the "real" (natural) science majors, such as myself, snickered at those who majored in the social sciences, and perhaps we humiliated them. The social sciences—anthropology, economics, history, political science, psychology, and sociology—lead to knowing about the structure of societies. Social sciences seem markedly less than precisely scientific when compared to the natural sciences. When the medical school of which I was later a faculty member attempted to introduce a social science program into the curriculum, once again the "real" scientists exclaimed their dismay and self-righteous disapproval. At the time, I was supportive of this curricular change. I now understand, however, that this led only to the students' having to *know* more about their patients and brought them not one whit closer to understanding their patients. We can know about the structure of societies of ants and bees without understanding ants and bees. It is folly merely to know about the structure of human society without understanding human nature.

One of many texts, read in solitude, that contributed to my own exploration was *The Life and Times of Chaucer* by John Gardner.[7] I sensed that although the people in Chaucer's time and culture existed in a way that was significantly different from how I exist, their perceptions, values, tastes, emotions, fantasies, desires, and impulses, their essence, had an altogether familiar ring. I also found their response to humiliation to be no different than the response to humiliation today. Times and cultures change; perhaps human nature does not.

THE HUMANITIES

It is in the humanities—art, classical language and literature, drama, English, modern languages and literature, music, philosophy, religion, and theology—that we find the essence of life. It is in the humanities that we find the stuff of the Who-Self. I have already addressed the importance of language in the expression of the Who-Self and will not add to that argument here other than to say that without language my human nature is not accessible and therefore not understandable to others.

There is, of course, learning and knowledge to be had in the humanities, but these are of little moment. One might, for example, dedicate time and effort to learning about and knowing about Brahms and might become the world's most learned expert on Brahms. Such a person, however, could never hear the Brahms

---

7. John Gardner, *The Life and Times of Chaucer* (New York: Vintage Books, 1978).

Double Concerto in A Minor through my ears. That experience is uniquely mine and belongs to my Who-Self, to my essence. My personal taste in art runs to Jan Vermeer and Paul Klee; this is an expression of my perceptions, my tastes, and my values—of my Who-Self. Knowing about art or knowing about Jan Vermeer or Paul Klee are distinctly different matters. And it is same with literature. I will once again refer to Whitehead, who wrote, "To this day I cannot read *King Lear,* having had the advantage of studying it accurately in school."[8] The beauty of *King Lear* comes from exploring it and understanding it, not from studying and knowing about it.

I return now to my earlier comments in this monograph concerning the chasm between the natural sciences and the humanities, the chasm that became evident to me in my undergraduate days. That chasm is real. It is the chasm between *knowing* about the nature of the universe through the natural sciences and *understanding* the nature of humanity through the humanities. It is the chasm between knowledge and wisdom. It is the natural distinction between the What-Self, which can be *known* through the natural sciences and the social sciences, and the Who-Self, which can be expressed and understood through language, art, drama, and music. The other disciplines of the humanities, namely, philosophy, religion, and theology, will be addressed in the final two sections of this chapter.

---

8. Alfred North Whitehead, *Atlantic,* Vol. 138, p. 197.

MEDICINE

Medicine's domain is knowledge about the non-choice What-Self body and, more precisely, the maintenance of a healthy existence for that body. But, often tragically, the physician's concern for existence becomes an obsession, and the essence of the patient is ignored. The surgeon, for example, may operate on my What-Self body and repair it, returning it to a state of healthy existence. But the surgeon cannot operate on my Who-Self, and if, in doing surgery, the surgeon ignores my Who-Self, my very essence is ignored.

There is an important ethical issue currently confronting medicine and society: When does a fetus become human? This question is as difficult as it is important. Consideration of this issue has led not to exploration and understanding but rather to expert What-Self camps each claiming to have the correct answer. One such camp champions a woman's right to choose to have an abortion. This reinforces the destructive view of what you do matters and who you are doesn't matter. Another camp champions the fetus's right to existence and ignores the right to life, to essence. I believe that the resolution of this ethical dilemma can only come from wisdom and not from debating facts and knowledge. Such wisdom might well include what I have come to understand about abortion. I have never found a mother (or father) who did not experience the procedure of abortion as humiliating, even when the decision for abortion was based on sound logic, reason, and considered judgment. For example if a woman is raped, the rape itself is an experience of humiliation. If she becomes pregnant in the rape, then choosing to have an abortion has an appealing logic to it, but the abortion adds yet another experience of humiliation.

In the service of a healthy existence, medicine often recommends to patients, and all too often in a manner that sounds like an order rather than a recommendation, that they should choose to experience something that feels unnatural. Being paraded naked before strangers, being dismembered, being disemboweled, being invaded by knives and tubes and instruments and needles, being hooked to or implanted with machines, being whisked away from one's home, giving birth in a brightly lighted public arena, being asked to present samples of urine and feces and sputum, being asked about one's private affairs—all of these events can and may be experienced as humiliating. If the patient sees the physician only as a What-Self and/or if the patient is seen only as a What-Self, the chance for humiliation is great. If the physician and patient see each other only as Who-Selves and can ignore their What-Selves, then they have an intimate, human Who-Self relationship, and humiliation is not possible. In this state, any and all procedures, however painful, can be done in love and understanding.

Somewhere along the way—the way to knowledge, not the way to understanding—I *learned* that people fear hospitals because they associate hospitals with death. Sickness and pain and death are all part of our natural existence. It is the nature of our What-Self existence to be born, to grow, to bear fruit, and to die. But it is not natural to be humiliated, and it is humiliation that people associate with hospitals and being humiliated in hospitals that they fear. Further, it is during the natural process of dying that physicians most often inflict the greatest acts of humiliation in their preoccupation with existence and their inattention to the essence of their patients.

As a What-Self physician and a sometimes What-Self patient, I do not in any way wish to demean physicians. If disembowelment is in order, I would be most grateful for my surgeon not only to be good enough, but to be very, very good and successful. But I do wish to point out the tragedy in our system of training physicians. To become a good enough What-Self physician one is expected to be an expert; in fact, during training one senses that one cannot be good enough until one *knows* everything. I had to learn about, know about, and be able to demonstrate my knowledge of the *flexor digiti quinti brevis,* a small muscle in the hand that is barely as long as its name. Long before they reach the practice of medicine, good enough students have learned that what you do matters and who you are doesn't matter. This learned nontruth is vigorously reinforced along the path to medical knowledge, on the path to becoming an expert, good enough What-Self physician. One can be successful at this while understanding nothing.

A final note on medicine involves the issue of technology. The advances in technology by expert What-Self scientists and physicians have led to the availability of, for example, mechanical hearts. Economists are telling society that we are reaching or have reached the point at which we cannot pay for these advances; our technology has outrun our resources. There is no particular wisdom in this, just facts. The mechanical heart can often prolong existence, and those physicians who are obsessed with existence may see a value in mechanical hearts, a value that does not match up with their cost. Of what value is prolonged existence without essence? It is my view that many mechanical heart recipients experience humiliation in the costly process of prolonging their existence. Perhaps choosing to have a mechanical heart is not all that different from Sophie's choice.

LAW

The law may be seen as the embodiment of a societal ethic in a system of rules of conduct. A primary societal ethic is that members of that society are expected to conduct themselves in a reasoned, timely, orderly fashion, and the code of law makes more or less explicit what is acceptable conduct. The law is dynamic and changes with time to reflect changes in societal ethics. Societies need be tolerant of some degree of social deviance, for without social deviance there is no social change, and without social change societies become rigid and stagnant.

Until the time of Greek civilization, the law was based primarily on the principle of an eye for an eye, a tooth for a tooth. On the basis of this principle, which finds its origin in the Code of Hammurabi, the law was the agent for revenge. In the Greek legend, Orestes was excused for killing his mother because he had been driven to the act in order to avenge his father's murder. This represents an historic point in the law of Western civilization in that it marks the first time that the law sanctioned an independent act of revenge by a citizen.

When one is accused of violating the law, of standing outside the societal ethic, the court of law has the task of deciding whether or not the law applies to the specific facts and circumstances of the specific case in question. Thus, it is the law, it is the societal ethic, that is really on trial. Through this process the law is modified to reflect more clearly the societal ethic. If, in this process, the accused is found guilty under the law, then that person may also be punished under the law. Therefore, the code of punishment also reflects societal ethics. The issue of punishment will be addressed more specifically in the next section.

My rationale for including the law in this commentary is to point out the limitations of the law. When found guilty and punished under the law, a person is held accountable to society as a What-Self member of that society. If the crime involves an act of humiliation, the law is impotent to resolve the victim's dilemma of despair or the humiliator's dilemma of shame. The law may order restitution to the victim, but this does not resolve the victim's dilemma, as has already been described with regard to Sophie's dilemma. The criminal acts of rape and kidnap are acts of humiliation against human nature as well as acts against the law. The current spate of international terrorism, beginning with the assault on the American Embassy in Tehran in 1979, also offers grim examples of humiliation no more or less devastating than Sophie's choice. Less dramatic acts of humiliation occur daily that are not acts against the law. The essential point is that the law has the authority and responsibility to find people guilty or not guilty under the law and to punish people under the law, but the law has no authority or ability to resolve the human dilemma. It is also true that judges and attorneys and juries, in their What-Self positions of authority and power, may, and sometimes do, humiliate people at the same time that they are acting in the service of justice.

The function of probate courts in their responsibility to minors offers another example of the limitations of the law. When there is evidence before the court of child neglect or child abuse, including physical, psychological, and sexual abuse, then the court often acts to take the child out of harm's way by placing him or her in protective custody, often in a foster home or group shelter. That the court has the responsibility to take the child out of harm's way seems clear. The child, in being neglected or abused by its parents, is being humiliated and thus alienated from its parents. To take the child out of the home is an appropriate reflection of societal ethics but does not resolve the alienation that is part of the dilemma. In fact, it magnifies the alienation. To remove the child is a humane act, but to leave the child stuck in the dilemma is not humane.

In summary, the court of law has the authority and responsibility to prosecute persons who violate the law and to punish such persons under the law when they are found guilty. In distinct contrast, the court has no power or authority to provide resolution of the dilemma that arises from violation of humanity in any act of humiliation. Indeed, there are many acts of humiliation, for example demeaning ethnic jokes, that occur daily and that do not violate the law.

PUNISHMENT

In hierarchical What-Self groups, such as families, businesses, organizations, schools, communities, governments, and societies, rules ensure that the group functions in an orderly fashion. I am quick to point out that families could be peaceful and happy and orderly in the absence of a What-Self hierarchy, but to be so family members would have to leave their What-Selves at the front door. For rules to have any effect they must be enforced by those in authority, and violations of rules must be met with penalties or punishments.

To avoid chaos, rules (What–Self measurements) must be explicit, fair, and uniformly applied. It follows that penalties or punishments must also be explicit, fair, and uniformly applied. When the rules and/or the penalties are not explicit, fair, and uniformly applied, chaos ensues.

That rules and penalties, measurements and consequences of not being good enough are necessary in the What–Self world seems evident. But being a responsible What–Self is foreign to the free, responsive Who–Self. It is natural for everyone—at least those who are clearly aware of who they are—to test the rules to make certain that the rules are real. If an employee chronically comes to work late or leaves early and nothing happens, then she or he understands that there is no real measurement for being timely at work. When a student consistently does very poor work and is advanced to the next grade without comment and is allowed to participate in sports, then he or she understands that there is no real measurement for academic success. Those who are in authority have the responsibility to enforce the rules. When this is not done or is not done consistently the rules are seen as not real and meaningless. It is much easier for the What–Self to function when one is certain that the rules and penalties are real.

The dynamics of this issue are easily found in the microcosm of adolescents, who vigorously and appropriately test the rules at home and at school to make certain that the rules are real. All too often, both at school and within the family, the rules are not explicit, fair, or uniformly applied. Equally as often, the rules are explicit but those in authority do not themselves enforce them, expecting the adolescents themselves to enforce them; this cannot work. How can one enforce the rules and test them at the same time? Furthermore, to make a rule that cannot possibly be enforced means that the rule isn't real.

Parents and teachers and school administrators often get very upset and make angry, self-righteous, judgmental pronouncements when adolescents do what they need to do, namely, test the rules. Being upset is a punishment for such parents, teachers, and administrators and not for the adolescents. If police officers merely got upset and yelled at citizens without ever issuing citations, many laws would go largely unheeded as not real. The very same parents, teachers, and administrators who bemoan the alleged unwieldiness of adolescents have themselves tested rules; for example, many drive more than 55 miles per hour (the current maximum by law in the United States) on the freeway. It is, in fact, reassuring to adolescents when they find, upon testing the rules, that the rules hold true.

Many adolescents who are seen as model teenagers have learned to be good enough What-Selves as a way to be loveable and loved. Such adolescents enforce others' (parents' and teachers') rules for themselves without ever testing them. They become model What-Selves who are afraid of their Who-Selves. They end up existing successfully, but rarely do they live.

Rules and penalties, when explicit, fair, and uniformly applied, make sense. If you score less than 75 on an examination, that's not good enough; you flunk. Fair enough. If you miss work without reason, you don't get paid; if you miss work too often, you get fired. Fair enough. If you let the parking meter elapse, you get a citation; if you don't pay the fine, you get a court summons. Fair enough. You have to be home from the dance by midnight or you lose the privilege to drive the family car for a week. Fair enough.

Penalties are one thing, but punishment is quite another. Punishment generally connotes retribution or getting even. Punishment often is an act of humiliation, and in my view any act of humiliation is an attack on civility and on humanity. Humiliation of one demeans each of us equally and magnifies human alienation and despair. Penalties are fair enough; humiliation is never fair. To my mind, nothing can possibly justify an act of humiliation—absolutely nothing.

If a child is forced to bare its bottom skyward for paddling, the child is humiliated, no matter how gentle the paddling and despite disclaimers such as "this hurts me more than it does you." If a student is ridiculed by a teacher in front of the class, the student is humiliated. If an employee is berated in front of his or her peers by a boss, the employee is humiliated.

And quite certainly being hanged in public, being beheaded in public, being drawn and quartered in public, or being put into the public stocks are humiliating.

Without penalties, rules are meaningless and impotent; without penalties, the law is meaningless and impotent. But when penalties or punishments involve humiliation, humanity and civility become meaningless and impotent. We demean our own humanness when we personally humiliate another or when we conspire as a member of society to humiliate another, even when that other has committed a most heinous crime. Therefore, to be a member of a society that condones humiliation in the penalizing or punishment of a rule breaker or a law breaker is to conspire against our very humanness. This would, perforce, include the use of capital punishment. When we accept capital punishment as just punishment, we demean ourselves. To quote from a press release of a recent speech by United States Supreme Court Justice William Brennan, capital punishment "treats members of the human race as nonhumans, as objects to be toyed with and discarded . . . The calculated killing of a human being by the state involves, by its very nature, an absolute denial of the executed person's humanity. . . A punishment must not be so severe as to be utterly and irreversibly degrading to the very essence of human dignity."

Returning to the model of Sophie's choice, one cannot ignore the SS doctor's act of humiliation, cannot approve of that act, and cannot forgive the SS doctor for that act. To me it is equally evident that some penalty and/or some act of contrition or penitence is in order. However, as has already been shown, there is no penalty that society can impose and no act of contrition or penitence that the SS doctor can do that would relieve Sophie of her dilemma. To humiliate the SS doctor in return, no matter how natural and human the desire to do so, would simply magnify the human dilemma. It is important to find a way to penalize the SS doctor for his act without humiliating him. It is of the utmost importance for the SS doctor and Sophie to be reconciled. This is important to all of us.

WAR AND PEACE

From the What-Self arises inequality and power. From inequality and power arises war.

In the Who-Self there is equality and irrevocable togetherness. In equality and togetherness there is peace.

PHILOSOPHY

In this section I will comment on how a number of philosophers or schools of philosophy pertain to a theory on the nature of humanity or how they might be understood through this theory. My comments are not offered as critical analyses of these philosophers and philosophies, but rather as a different perspective on historical philosophical thought.

Lao-tze

Lao-tze lived in China in the fifth century before Christ. Near the time of his death he wrote the *Tao Te Ching,* which was the distillation of his thought and wisdom. Lao-tze's views may be seen as pure expressions of the Who-Self and oblivious to the What-Self. His writings reflect solitude, intimacy, and being at one with nature. The only forces that Lao-tze recognizes are natural forces, and he speaks against the unnatural forces arising from the power of What-Selves. I have quoted from the writings of Lao-tze earlier in this monograph and now offer one final quotation which, in my view, makes perfect sense from the perspective of the distinction between Who-Self and What-Self:

> Many say the following of Tao is the way of a fool.
> If it were not the way of a fool,
> It would not be so simple.
> If it were the way of the learned,
> It would have vanished long ago,
> Buried under rules and definitions.
>
> Those known as fools may lack knowledge,
> But knowledge is not wisdom.
> Even the ignorant can understand this,
> Yet those of learning do not.[9]

K'ung Fu-tze (Confucius)

K'ung Fu-tze was a younger contemporary of Lao-tze. K'ung Fu-tze focused almost exclusively on the

9. In Benjamin Hoff, *The Way to Life* (New York: John Weatherhill, Inc., 1981), p. 46.

What-Self, prescribing systems of classifying people as superior or inferior, rules (measurements), hierarchies, a rational basis for conduct, and the responsibilities of the What-Self. He dealt with the unnatural What-Self world of hierarchy, responsibility, power, and a reasoned good versus bad, whereas Lao-tze experienced the natural world of being at one with nature in freedom, peace, and love.

Socrates

Socrates lived in the century following Lao-tze and K'ung Fu-tze. What little is known of Socrates comes from Plato's recording of the *Dialogues,* in which Socrates portrays himself as a common, uneducated man. Socrates was a man of questions. In his questioning he demanded of others that they be exact in their definitions of words. (We now refer to the method of teaching that is based on questioning as the Socratic method.) A major theme of the *Dialogues* is the distinction between intelligence and wisdom. It was Socrates who said "know thyself" (Who-Self?). According to tradition, when asked who was the wisest man in Greece, the oracle at Delphi replied "Socrates." In response to this, Socrates said of himself that the only thing he knew was that he knew nothing. While struggling with the questions of wisdom and virtue, he exemplified the distinction between knowledge and wisdom, between the Who-Self and What-Self.

According to the accounts of Plato, Socrates was charged with corrupting the youth of the city and with rejecting the gods of Athens and introducing new divinities and sentenced to death. In 399 B.C. when, at the age of 70, he accepted the deadly cup of hemlock, he told his friends to be of good cheer and say that they were burying his body only. He accepted death, the end of existence, with the same dignity as Lao-tze. It is a challenge to one's imagination to contemplate the depth and richness of wisdom that might have emerged from a dialogue between these two wise men, Socrates and Lao-tze.

Plato

Socrates was a common man, whereas Plato was of the aristocracy. That Plato's life and thought were touched deeply by his association with Socrates is beyond doubt. Plato attempted to design a Utopian state in which all Men would be equal, but the design was based on the development of a What-Self ruling class, thereby ensuring inequality and a basis for power. Further, the ruling class was to be developed through rigorous education, thereby making the ruling class knowledgeable and learned but not necessarily wise. Education can be legislated, wisdom cannot. Plato stands as an exemplary model of a brilliant mind at work, but intellectual brilliance is not a substitute for understanding and wisdom. Plato became the foundation of philosophy for Western civilization, and that foundation is firmly embedded in our intellect and reason in the service of knowing about our What-Self world of existence. Although intellectualization and rationalization have come to be understood as psychological defense mechanisms, philosophy in

Western civilization remains by-and-large wedded to rational thinking and consequently is divorced from the essence of life and wisdom.

Aristotle

Aristotle was Plato's pupil, and the student was the intellectual match of the master. Aristotle's father was a physician, and Aristotle himself may have studied and practiced medicine. In any case, Aristotle joined the Academy at Athens when Plato was in his sixty-first year, and soon Plato saw Aristotle as the shining intellect of the Academy. Aristotle, with his medical background, brought science to philosophy. He systematized Plato's thoughts, he founded the science of biology, and he reinforced philosophy's foundation of intellect and reason by adding formal logic. His motto was *nil admirari,* "admire nothing." I would modify this to "know everything, experience nothing." In saying that Man is by nature a political animal, Aristotle places the nature of Man in the What-Self and further obscures the essence of the Who-Self. Central to Greek philosophy was the question of the nature of being. After answering all other questions with reason and logic, Greek philosophy could not answer this question.

St. Augustine

Augustine was born in 354 A.D. in the Roman province of Numidia in North Africa. Even as a young boy he was recognized as a capable student, and he became well educated. He was learned in philosophy

and rhetoric. At the age of 30 he accepted the chair
of rhetoric in Milan, Italy, where he came to know St.
Ambrose and at the same time he began reading the
Neo-Platonists. The history of the remainder of his
life, including his famous writings, can be best understood as a struggle to make his keenly aware Who-Self
compatible with knowledge. Augustine struggled
hard and long in his quest for truth, but claimed to
be hindered by the reason and logic of having read
the books of the Platonists. Despite the powerful experiences of his Who-Self, Augustine focused on the
What-Self good-bad dichotomy. Given the foundations of Western thought and philosophy, it is not
surprising that Augustine took the stand that there
can be no conflict between faith and reason, that God's
knowledge is divine knowledge, that angels are intellectual beings, and that humans are rational beings.

The life of St. Augustine has been described as a
spiritual (Who-Self) and intellectual (What-Self) pil-
grimage. Initially he sought a philosophy of truth
through reason, but eventually he came to the view
that it is only through faith and revelation that Man
can become rational, that it is only through faith and
revelation that Man can become a philosopher. This
is found in the Augustinian principle *crede ut intellegas*
or "believe to understand." This makes perfect sense
if understanding is equated with wisdom coming from
exploration rather than with rational, logical knowledge coming from learning. However, Augustine's
impact on the Western Latin Church and on Western

civilization was to indelibly wed faith with reason. If faith and revelation enables Man's reason, as Augustine posits, can this reason answer the question of the nature of being, the question left unanswered by Plato and Aristotle? And can this reason distinguish between existence and essence? To my mind, the answer to both of these questions must be no.

St. Thomas Aquinas

Thomas Aquinas was born near Naples, Italy nearly 800 years after the death of St. Augustine. At age five he was sent to the Abbey of Monte Casino where he remained for nine years receiving his early education. Later he became a Dominican friar, and at the age of twenty he began his training in theology at the Dominican convent in Paris. At the age of twenty-seven he began his career as teacher and writer, and these activities were his ministry until his death at the age of forty-nine.

Aquinas, through his teacher Albert the Great, became imbued with the science and logic of Aristotle, which brought him into conflict with, amongst others, the Augustinians, who took exception to the application of Aristotlian principles to theology. As Augustine had brought Plato to the Western Latin Church, in a similar manner Aquinas brought Aristotle to the Church. Aquinas, as the foremost apologist of the Church during the Middle Ages, advanced the view that reason and logic, based in Aristotle, could lead to a true knowledge of the world and of God.

In contrast to Augustine, Aquinas saw that faith and revelation directed reason but did not have to precede reason. Aquinas made three disclaimers to his view that reason could suffice as a path to knowledge of God: first, that Man was too lazy or too preoccupied with secular affairs to use his reason; second, that true philosophy required many years of diligent study so that only a few rare elderly people could reach the knowledge of God; and third, that Man's inherent weakness of intellect made revelation more efficient than reason although Man, through reason, should be able to reach a knowledge of God. With this view Aquinas set about to apply Aristotelian categories to every domain of existing knowledge. In his *Summa Theologica,* he raises all possible questions regarding the nature of God and the nature of Man and answers each question with precise, masterful logic and reason. This work became the foundation of theology for the Western Latin Church. In it, Aquinas meets the question of being, the unanswered question of the Greek philosophers, head on. In Question 13, Article II of the *Summa Theologica* Aquinas states, "I answer that, this name, HE WHO IS, is most properly applied to God. . .it does not signify form, but being itself. Hence since the being of God is His essence itself, which can be said of no other, it is clear that among other names this one specifically names God." I would suggest that being, essence, and the Who-Self are commutable.

On December 6, 1273 Aquinas, while celebrating mass, experienced something that came over him.

Church historians have typically described it as a mystical experience. After this experience, Aquinas ceased writing and, when urged by a colleague to continue writing, he is said to have responded, "I can do no more. Such things have been revealed to me that all I have written seems as straw."[10] I would suggest that this experience, just three months before Thomas's death, was an experience of the Who-Self that had nothing to do with logic or reason.

Francis Bacon

Francis Bacon lived from 1561 to 1626 with careers in both politics and philosophy. At age twelve Bacon went to Cambridge, England, where he spent three years. He came away from Cambridge with an avowed disdain for educational systems in general and with Aristotelian philosophy in particular. He aspired to change philosophy from a form of theoretical musings to a force of change in society. Bacon set about with the view that observation and inductive reason in science could subdue nature and that putting science in control would lead to Utopia. He maintained that knowledge and human power were synonymous. Bacon thus came down squarely on the side of knowledge and science, and in so doing he did considerable service to the natural sciences. He also gave direction to British thought, his work leading directly to

---

10. *Thomas Aquinas: I,* No. 19 of *Great Books of the Western World,* Robert Maynard Hutchins, editor-in-chief (Chicago, Ill.: Encyclopaedia Britannica, Inc., 1952), p. vi.

Thomas Hobbes's materialism and John Locke's empiricism. Bacon defined three grades of human ambition, the highest of which was to "endeavor to renew and enlarge the power and empire of mankind in general over the universe."[11] His philosophy of better existence through science, or "better living through chemistry" as the contemporary slogan goes, gives no heed to the essence of life.

René Descartes

Descartes was born in France in 1596 when Bacon was age thirty-five. Idealistic and subjective, he provided the opposite view of Bacon's realism and objectivity. Descartes's early education was with the Jesuit religious order. He eventually received a degree in law from the University of Poitiers, after which he studied algebra and geometry. He became highly regarded as a scientist and mathematician, but it was his view of the primacy of consciousness and his famous dictum *Cogito, ergo sum* ("I think therefore I am") that led to his being seen as a philosopher. Descartes wished to explain the world, except for the soul (Who-Self?) and God (Who-Self?), by the laws of mathematics and physics. He advanced a particularly important concept that there is a homogeneous substance underlying all forms of matter and a different homogeneous substance underlying all forms of mind.

---

11. "Novum Organum," first book, in *Francis Bacon,* No. 30 of *Great Books of the Western World,* Robert Maynard Hutchins, editor-in-chief (Chicago, Ill.: Encyclopaedia Britannica, Inc., 1952), p. 135.

Baruch Spinoza

In 1632, six years after the death of Bacon and in Descartes's thirty-sixth year, Baruch Spinoza was born in Amsterdam, Holland. Even as a young boy he was perceived as intellectually gifted, but his curiosity (desire to explore) led to questioning and to the development of unorthodox views. In 1656 he was charged with heresy by the elders of his synagogue, and on refusing to recant his views he was excommunicated with full ritual. He later studied Latin, saw no valid distinction between the Old and New Testament, and saw Judaism and Christianity as one religion. Following his excommunication and his estrangement from his family, Spinoza lived simply and supported himself at the trade of lens grinder. He was influenced by the writings of Descartes and himself wrote a tract entitled *Descartes' Principles of Philosophy Geometrically Demonstrated.* Spinoza's writings have been seen as complex and controversial and have been subject to much varied interpretation, but only one aspect of Spinoza's philosophy needs be considered here. Spinoza's system of philosophy is based on three terms: substance, attribute, and mode. The concept of substance draws on Descartes's notion of a homogeneous substance underlying all forms of mind and matter. Spinoza identified substance with that which is, with being, with nature, and with God. In the context of a theory on the nature of humanity, Descartes's substance further defined by Spinoza may be seen as the Who-Self.

John Locke

John Locke was born in England in 1632, the same year that Spinoza was born. Locke's *Essay on Human Understanding* began an introspective, psychological movement in philosophy. Locke stated that all knowledge comes from experience and through one's senses. Locke concluded that all we can *know* is matter, since it is matter that affects the senses. He further concluded that philosophy must, perforce, be a materialistic philosophy (nothing exists except matter) of empiricism (knowledge comes only through experience). Locke was concerned primarily with political issues, but his philosophical views were quite threatening to the established orthodoxy of religion. Yet Locke always saw himself as a good Christian and, near the end of his long life, he wrote a commentary on St. Paul's Epistles. In the absence of a visible God of matter, the church feared that Locke's philosophy would lead to an assault on the belief in God.

George Berkley

George Berkley (1685–1753), a much younger contemporary of Locke, was an Anglican priest in Ireland and, near the end of his life, became Bishop of Cloyne. In studying philosophy, Berkley found Locke's principles difficult to accept, and in the early 1700s he set forth a new philosophical principle that turned round the Lockian view. Berkley claimed that Locke's work actually demonstrated that the only reality was in the mind, that all matter was, in fact, a condition of the mind. Berkley's principle, which elevated mind over matter, would, if accepted, lay materialism to rest.

David Hume

David Hume (1711–1776) was born in Scotland at about the time that Berkley was setting forth his unique philosophical views. During a three-year sojourn in France (he was not a collier), Hume wrote the *Treatise on Human Nature,* which was published in 1739. Hume met Berkley's principle of the mind head on with the view that the mind does not exist and cannot be known; that the concept of the mind is merely an abstraction for a disconnected series of perceived thoughts, ideas, feelings, and memories. Thus, as Berkley's view had apparently destroyed the concept of matter with the concept of mind, Hume apparently destroyed the concept of mind. His view also disallowed the concept of a soul. Hume left philosophy empty of substance. He went further with his principle of perceptions and sequences of events to state that there were no natural laws, that such laws are merely mental manipulations of sequences of perceptions into mental generalizations and classifications. Therefore, the laws of science are internal events of the human mind and not laws intrinsic to nature. Hume's views put the very foundations of science and philosophy at the risk of being destroyed.

Immanuel Kant

Immanuel Kant (1724–1804) was born, lived, and died in Königsberg, East Prussia. He attended university as a theology student but his primary interest was in the sciences, specifically in mathematics and physics. His great contribution was to come not in science but in metaphysics, beginning with the publication of *Critique of Pure Reason* in 1781. In 1775 Kant had read the German translation of Hume's works. Kant's writings were extraordinarily complex and a wellspring of philosophical controversy throughout the nineteenth century. What is of concern here is that Kant, in taking clear, explicit exception to Hume and the English school of philosophy, demonstrated that the world is only known to us through sensations, and that the mind actively processes these sensations rather than passively receives them. With this view Kant, who came from a Puritan religious background, was able to reconcile philosophy with a religious view. German Idealism, with its genesis in Kant, affected not only the thought of the nineteenth century, but indeed the very culture of Europe.

William James

William James was born in New York city in 1842. As a young man James, in private schools in America and in Europe, studied in the natural sciences, received a medical degree from Harvard, and in 1872 was appointed to the faculty of Harvard as instructor in physiology. He remained a member of the Harvard faculty the remainder of his life. He first taught physiology and anatomy, then psychology, and finally philosophy. His first and most famous work, *The Principles of Psychology,* was published in 1890, but from 1900 onward all of his writings were in philosophy. While James's psychology was metaphysical, his philosophy was clearly pragmatic and focused on the consequences of thought rather than on the origin of thought. He reacted to the idealism and metaphysics of Kant and the German School of philosophy with scientific empiricism and realism. He studied from both sides of the chasm, from the perspective of the natural sciences on one side and the perspective of the humanities on the other. He looked into the chasm but never explained it. Near his death he wrote, "There is no conclusion."

Existentialism

The effects of existentialism on twentieth century philosophy and theology will be addressed in greater depth in a subsequent monograph. Here I will merely point out a principle of existentialism as it relates to a theory on the nature of humanity. Existentialism in all its forms holds that existence precedes essence. The theory offered herein presents the view that existence, the What-Self, and essence, the Who-Self, develop simultaneously through the processes of separation, leading to existence, and individuation, leading to essence. For the individual human being, existence and essence coincide; one does not precede the other. To an observer, a human being may be seen as matter, as living matter, or as male or female *Homo sapiens*. Such observation reveals no more than the observation of other living matter, of, for example, a male or female horse. To the observer, the observed *Homo sapiens* appears no different before, during, or after the process of separation-individuation, appears no different before existence and essence than it does after the emergence of existence and essence.

Alfred North Whitehead

Alfred North Whitehead (1861–1947) may or may not join the ranks of the great philosophers of Western civilization. That is of little consequence for he is included here as a matter of personal taste, as an expression of my Who-Self. With the exception of Plato's *Republic,* Whitehead's works, which I read in high school, were my first introduction to philosophy. I made (and make) no pretense of understanding Whitehead's philosophy, but in his writings I found something warm and human and exciting. Without being able to point to anything specific, I am aware that my experience with Whitehead's writings is woven into the very fabric of the theory on the nature of humanity.

Whitehead was born in England. His father was an Anglican priest, his grandfather was an educator. Whitehead had a classical education and then sat for a degree in mathematics at Cambridge. His academic career at Cambridge was exclusively in mathematics, but he engaged in scholarly discourse with other students and faculty in a variety of settings. During his undergraduate days he became familiar with philosophical traditions including those of Kant. He stayed on at Cambridge until 1910, when he joined the faculty at the University of London. In 1924 he was appointed professor of philosophy at Harvard, where he finished out his teaching career.

He believed that every human being mattered, and he believed that Man could live in peace. I would like to believe that he understood that being who you are matters and doing what you do doesn't matter. I would indicate here a quotation from Whitehead which, in my view, is consistent with a theory on the nature of humanity: "Religion is what the individual does with his own solitariness."[12]

I will conclude this section on philosophy with yet another quote from Whitehead: "Philosophy begins in wonder. And, at the end, when philosophic thought has done its best, the wonder remains. There have been added, however, some grasp of the immensity of things, some purification of emotion by understanding."[13]

THEOLOGY

God is!

God is Who. One cannot see God, cannot touch God, cannot know God, and cannot make statements about God, other than God is. One can only understand and accept God. God is essence, not existence. In our Who-Self essence, in our solitude and intimacy, we are separate and equal and together with all other

12. Alfred North Whitehead, *Religion in the Making* (New York: Macmillan Co., 1926), p. 16.

13. Alfred North Whitehead, *Modes of Thought* (New York: Macmillan Co., 1938), p. 232.

Who-Selves and we are *with* God. God has no What-Self, is not Man, is not male or female, is not out there or up there. God simply is.

"And God said unto Moses, I AM THAT I AM: and he said, Thus shalt thou say unto the children of Israel, I AM hath sent me unto you" (Exodus 3:14).[14]

The peace of God is the peace of Eden, the peace of solitude, the peace of intimacy, the peace of the nothingness of the Tao. As Who-Selves we are peaceful and free and joyous, we can be neither powerful or powerless, we can be neither rejected nor humiliated. In solitude and intimacy we experience God, we experience Eden, we experience the way of nothingness. We are wise without knowledge. Adam saw (experienced) every creature *before* he named it. Adam was with God in Eden, with God in solitude before Eve, and with God in intimacy after Eve.

"And the LORD God commanded the man, saying, Of every tree of the garden thou mayest freely eat; but of the tree of *knowledge* of good and evil, thou shalt not eat of it: for in the day that thou eatest thereof thou shalt surely die" (Genesis 2:16–17; italics mine).

And, of course, Adam and Eve did eat of the tree of knowledge and in their choice to *know* became What-Selves leading to explainability, measurability, inequality, power, and the risk of rejection and humiliation. And God measured them and said, "what is

---

14. This and all following biblical quotations are from the King James Version.

this that thou hast done?... And I will put enmity
between thee and the woman... Because thou hast
harkened unto the voice of thy wife, and hast eaten
of the tree [of knowledge], of which I have commanded thee, saying, Thou shalt not eat of it: cursed
is the ground for thy sake; in sorrow shalt thou eat
of it [knowledge] all the days of thy life... In the
sweat of thy face shalt thou eat bread... Behold, the
man is become as one of us, to *know* good and evil:
and now lest he put out his hand, and take also of the
tree of life, and eat, and live for ever: Therefore the
LORD God sent him forth from the garden of Eden,
to till the ground from whence he was taken" (Genesis
3:13–23; italics and brackets mine).

Adam and Eve were first of all Who-Selves without
knowledge of What-Selves, and experienced the essence of life in solitude and intimacy with God in
Eden. Once they ate from the tree of knowledge, they
became What-Selves, became responsible for their existence, and became alienated from God. This was the
end of the peaceful, equal essence of life. "And they
were both naked, the man and his wife, and were not
ashamed" (Genesis 2:25). After eating from the tree
of knowledge they were given responsibility for their
existence as What-Selves. Thus ended the peace of
Eden, and the war of the What-Selves began. "I will
put enmity between thee and the woman."

But Eden, being with God, is still available to Men
as Who-Selves oblivious to What-Selves in solitude
and intimacy. Theologians of the past century have

moved away from a What-Self concept of God out there and up there and have begun to explore for the essence of a WHO God in the depths of humanity. Martin Buber, Søren Kierkegaard, Dietrich Bonhoeffer, Karl Barth, Paul Tillich, Alfred North Whitehead, and Bishop John A. T. Robinson have all explored for the essence of God.

Bishop Robinson said, "To believe in God as love means to believe that in pure personal relationship we encounter, not merely what ought to be, but what is, the deepest, veriest truth about the structure of reality."[15] Here I would interpret Robinson's "pure personal relationship" as two (or more) Who-Selves in intimacy and with God.

Humis means earth. Having been taken from the earth and *being* with the earth in Eden, Adam is a Who-Self characterized by *humi*lity. As a What-Self existing outside Eden, Adam is at the risk of *humi*liation, of having his face pushed into the earth. In the natural state of the Who-Self experience of the essence of life, we are with the earth (*hum*ble). In the natural process of death, we return to the earth. While in the unnatural state of the What-Self, we are at risk of *humi*liation, of having our face rubbed in the dirt.

In solitude and intimacy, in Eden with God, it is possible to *do* anything, and the doing does not have to be reasoned or knowing. Thus it is possible to *do* what blacksmiths or physicians or cooks do in Eden,

---

15. John A. T. Robinson, *Honest to God* (Philadelphia, Penn.: Westminster Press, 1963), p. 49.

but without being a What-Self blacksmith or physician or cook. It is doing things naturally and freely from exploration and experience rather than doing things on the basis of learning and knowledge.

One final word on humiliation. In Sophie's choice, the SS doctor acted as a What-Self and saw Sophie only as a What-Self, leading to Sophie's humiliation and despair and to his own state of shame. "I will put enmity between thee and the woman." They were alienated one from the other and alienated from God. As long as Sophie sees the SS doctor only as a What-Self, she remains alienated, she remains stuck in the dilemma. If Sophie can experience herself for who she is and ignore what she is, if she can see the SS doctor for who he is and ignore what he is, she can be reconciled and thus become free of the dilemma. She can return to the peace of Eden. If she can see herself in the nakedness of her Who-Self and the SS doctor in the nakedness of his Who-Self, she can then reenter Eden. "And they were both naked... and were not ashamed."

That *A Theory on the Nature of Humanity* provides a different perspective for theological thought seems evident to me. I will attempt to explore the nature of God in the context of the nature of humanity in another monograph.

God is. You are. I am.

Peace be unto you.

Suggested Reading List

Auden, W. H. *Kierkegaard*. London: Cassell and Company, Ltd., 1955.

Barrette, Roy. *A Countryman's Journal*. Chicago: Rand McNally and Company, 1981.

Beston, Henry. *Northern Farm*. New York: Rinehart and Company, Inc., 1948.

Blythe, Ronald. *Akenfield*. New York: Pantheon Books, 1980.

Bonhoeffer, Dietrich. *The Cost of Discipleship*. New York: Macmillan Company, 1963.

_____. *Letters and Papers from Prison*. New York: Macmillan Company, 1967.

Buber, Martin. *I and Thou*. New York: Charles Scribner's Sons, 1958.

Burchfield, Robert. *The English Language*. Oxford: Oxford University Press, 1985.

Fromm, Erich. *Escape from Freedom*. New York: Holt, Rinehart and Winston, 1941.

_____. *The Sane Society*. New York: Holt, Rinehart and Winston. 1955

Gardner, John. *The Life and Times of Chaucer*. New York: Vintage Books, 1978.

Gathorne-Hardy, Jonathan. *The Unnatural History of the Nanny*. New York: Dial Press, 1973.

Hoff, Benjamin. *The Tao of Pooh*. New York: Penguin Books, 1983.

_____. *The Way to Life*. New York: John Weatherhill, Inc., 1981.

Mahler, Margaret; Pine, Fred; and Bergman, Anni. *The Psychological Birth of the Human Infant*. New York: Basic Books, Inc., 1975.

Maslow, Abraham H. *Motivation and Personality*. 2nd ed. New York: Harper and Row, Publishers, 1970.

_____. *Toward a Psychology of Being*. New York: D. Van Nostrand Company, 1968.

Masterson, James F. *The Narcissistic and Borderline Disorders*. New York: Brunner/Mazel, Publishers, 1981.

_____. *Psychotherapy of the Borderline Adult*. New York: Brunner/Mazel, Publishers, 1976.

_____. *The Real Self*. New York: Brunner/Mazel, Publishers, 1985

_____. *Treatment of the Borderline Adolescent: A Developmental Approach*. New York: John Wiley and Sons, Inc., 1972.

Mayerhoff, Milton. *On Caring*. New York: Harper and Row, Publishers, 1971.

Niebuhr, Reinhold. *The Nature and Destiny of Man*. New York: Charles Scribner's Sons, 1947.

Robinson, John A. T. *Honest to God*. Philadelphia, Penn.: Westminster Press, 1963.

Smedes, Lewis B. *Forgive and Forget*. San Francisco: Harper and Row, Publishers, Inc., 1984.

Tillich, Paul. *The Courage to Be*. New Haven, Conn.: Yale University Press, 1952.

_____. *The New Being*. New York: Charles Scribner's Sons, 1955.

Whitehead, Alfred North. *The Aims of Education*. New York: Macmillan Company, 1929.

_____. *Modes of Thought*. New York: Macmillan Company, 1938.

_____. *Religion in the Making*. New York: Macmillan Company, 1926.

A THEORY ON THE NATURE OF HUMANITY

Edited, designed, and
manufacture coordinated by
REDACTIONS UNLIMITED
East Lansing, Michigan

.

Typeset in
Mergenthaler's contemporary version of
BEMBO,
a typeface originally designed and cut by
Aldus Manutius in 1495

.

Composed by
PROFESSIONAL COMPOSITION, INC.
East Lansing, Michigan

.

Printed and bound by
BRAUN-BRUMFIELD, INC.
Ann Arbor, Michigan